BACK TO BASICS

MICHAEL SMITH
BACK TO BASICS
100 Simple Classic Recipes with a Twist

PHOTOGRAPHY BY RYAN SZULC

PENGUIN
an imprint of Penguin Canada

Published by the Penguin Group
Penguin Group (Canada), 90 Eglinton Avenue East, Suite 700,
Toronto, Ontario, Canada M4P 2Y3

Penguin Group (USA) Inc., 375 Hudson Street, New York, New York 10014, U.S.A.
Penguin Books Ltd, 80 Strand, London WC2R 0RL, England
Penguin Ireland, 25 St Stephen's Green, Dublin 2, Ireland (a division of Penguin Books Ltd)
Penguin Group (Australia), 707 Collins Street, Melbourne, Victoria 3008, Australia
(a division of Pearson Australia Group Pty Ltd)
Penguin Books India Pvt Ltd, 11 Community Centre, Panchsheel Park, New Delhi – 110 017, India
Penguin Group (NZ), 67 Apollo Drive, Rosedale, Auckland 0632, New Zealand
(a division of Pearson New Zealand Ltd)
Penguin Books (South Africa) (Pty) Ltd, 24 Sturdee Avenue, Rosebank,
Johannesburg 2196, South Africa
Penguin Books Ltd, Registered Offices: 80 Strand, London WC2R 0RL, England

First published 2013

1 2 3 4 5 6 7 8 9 10 (CR)

Copyright © Michael Smith, 2013

Food photography by Ryan Szulc
Food styling by Noah Witenoff
Prop styling by Madeleine Johari
Photos on pages viii–ix, x, and xii–xiii by James Ingram, Jive Photographic

Manufactured in the U.S.A.

Library and Archives Canada Cataloguing in Publication
Smith, Michael
Back to basics : 100 simple classic recipes with a twist / Michael Smith.
Includes index.

ISBN 978-0-14-318410-2

1. Cooking. 2. Cookbooks. I. Title.

TX714.S596 2013   641.5   C2013-900609-5

Visit the Penguin Canada website at **www.penguin.ca**

Special and corporate bulk purchase rates available; please see www.penguin.ca/corporatesales
or call 1-800-810-3104, ext. 2477.

ALWAYS LEARNING   PEARSON

This book is for anyone who likes to play in the kitchen,
for all who realize that recipes are more than just a destination,
they're a journey.

Also by

MICHAEL SMITH

Open Kitchen

The Inn Chef

Chef at Home

The Best of Chef at Home

Chef Michael Smith's Kitchen

Fast Flavours

CONTENTS

INTRODUCTION

When I was knee-high to a grasshopper, my mom welcomed me into her kitchen and without even realizing it began teaching me one of the most important lessons I've ever learned. The kitchen can be a friendly, relaxed place where at any moment magic can appear. Frankly, I think her intention was more to keep an eye on my brothers and me, but nevertheless I learned early on to enjoy myself in her kitchen.

Professional kitchens are dramatically different from home kitchens, but my mom's lesson has served me well throughout my career as a chef. I learned that hard work is its own reward and that no matter how serious the kitchen is, cooks will always find a way to stir in some fun. I learned a few more lessons along the way: that the cook matters a lot more than the recipe, that cooking does not have to be rigid, that recipes are really just a starting point.

Today, though, it's all about the realities of my family's kitchen. My job is to prepare multiple healthy, tasty meals every single day. My only real critics are my kids, and the end always justifies the means. In other words, as long as they're licking the plate clean I'm free to keep having fun in the kitchen.

You don't have to freestyle to be a great cook, but why not try? You can reliably stick to the basics of the recipes in this book, but you can just as easily find a way to stir in your own personality. Success is defined not by whether you cook exactly the way I do but by whether you and your table are enjoying yourselves. Nothing is more fun than taking pride in something you created yourself, then taking a bow for the inevitable compliments!

From gathering impeccable ingredients and learning the story of their provenance, to immersing yourself in the intricacies of a preparation, to triumphantly sharing the results, cooking can be a journey of discovery and fun. All you have to do is throw caution to the winds and relax!

SALADS

SALADS

GARDEN SALAD & A JAR OF HOUSE DRESSING

A homemade salad on the table is a great start to any meal—and to this book. Here's how to transform what you have on hand into a simple classic salad complete with your own improvised House Dressing. **SERVES A TABLE OF 4 TO 6 OR MORE**

For the greens

6 ounces (170 g) of fresh mixed greens, baby spinach, arugula, or mâche

A head or two of romaine, leaf, Bibb, or iceberg lettuce, chopped or torn

For the garnishes

A carrot or two, shredded

A stalk or two of celery, diced or shredded

Shredded red cabbage

1 or 2 crisp apples or pears, thinly sliced or shredded

A handful of shredded or sliced radishes

A handful or three of bean sprouts

A red onion, thinly sliced

A few green onions, thinly sliced

Handfuls of fresh basil, parsley, or mint leaves

For the dressing

½ cup (125 mL) or so of your very best extra-virgin olive oil

¼ cup (60 mL) or so of your favorite vinegar, any kind

¼ cup (60 mL) of honey, maple syrup, brown sugar, jam, jelly, or marmalade

A heaping tablespoon (18 mL) or so of Dijon or yellow mustard

A heaping tablespoon (18 mL) or so of your favorite spice, fresh or dried herb, or seasoning

To craft your own house salad, fill a festive salad bowl with handfuls of greens for everyone.

Choose from one or more of your favorite types of greens and feel free to create your own blend.

For lots of color and crunch, garnish your salad with a few of your favorite fruits and vegetables.

Now create your own House Dressing. It's just as easy to make a lot as a little, so fill a large jar to give you enough for this salad and a few more too. Choose an oil, something sour, something sweet, and a seasoning. Don't leave out the mustard—its unique binding properties will magically emulsify the works into a smooth dressing.

Shake, shake, shake until smooth, then pour a few spoonfuls of your magnificent House Dressing onto the salad, just enough to lightly coat the works. (You'll have lots of leftover dressing.) Quickly and gently toss the greens and garnishes together with the dressing until the salad feels evenly combined.

For maximum crisp and crunch, sprinkle the salad with any of these toppings: croutons, nuts, seeds, grains, dried fruit, granola, coarsely crushed tortilla chips.

TWIST

Your own simple homemade dressing masterpiece will easily beat any store-bought dressing and you'll enjoy the satisfaction of knowing you made it yourself as you bypass the pre-made "dressings" at the supermarket. Each of the ingredient categories is ripe for the creative picking too. Give some thought to your many options and you'll see the infinite possibilities in a simple salad. Maybe that's the real goal: filling your salad bowl with nourishment for the mind, body, *and* soul.

CAESAR SALAD
WITH A FEW TWISTS

When Caesar Cardini invented his salad in 1924, he had no idea how iconic it would become or that it would become our seemingly sole source of anchovies. Today it's a powerfully flavored classic that still inspires many ingenious garnish twists. SERVES 4

For the croutons

2 tablespoons (30 mL) of olive oil

2 garlic cloves, sliced

4 thick slices of rustic white bread, cubed or torn

2 tablespoons (30 mL) of water

For the pancetta crisps

12 thin slices of pancetta

For the dressing

1 head of garlic, cloves separated and peeled

A 2-ounce (50 g) can of anchovies, undrained

1½ cups (375 mL) of your very best extra-virgin olive oil

¼ cup (60 mL) of Dijon mustard

2 tablespoons (30 mL) of honey

1 tablespoon (15 mL) of Worcestershire sauce

The zest and juice of 3 lemons

For the salad

1 large head of romaine lettuce, torn and rinsed

Leaves from 1 large bunch of basil, torn

½ cup (125 mL) of genuine Grana Padano or Parmesan cheese, thinly sliced with a vegetable peeler

Salt and freshly ground pepper

Start with the croutons. Set your oven racks in the upper third and lower third of the oven. Preheat your oven to 375°F (190°C) and turn on your convection fan if you have one.

Splash the olive oil into a small saucepan over medium-high heat and toss in the garlic. Gently sizzle and stir, infusing the oil with the flavor of the garlic, 2 or 3 minutes. Strain out the garlic and remove the fragrant oil from the heat.

Put the bread cubes in a large mixing bowl, then vigorously toss them while evenly sprinkling with the water. Continue to toss while sprinkling with the olive oil, knowing that the water will ensure the croutons' interior chewiness while the oil will guarantee exterior crispness. Scatter them in a single even layer on a baking sheet and toast on the oven's higher rack until thoroughly golden brown, 15 to 20 minutes.

Meanwhile, make the pancetta crisps. To speed cleanup, line a baking sheet with parchment paper. Place the pancetta slices neatly on the tray without touching each other. Bake on the lower rack until the edges curl up and they're crispy like bacon, about 20 minutes. Drain on paper towels. If you like, carefully scrape out the delicious rendered fat and reserve it for the dressing.

For the dressing, fill your blender or food processor with the garlic, anchovies, oil, mustard, honey, Worcestershire sauce, and lemon zest and juice. Add the pancetta fat if you like. Process the works to a smooth dressing.

Wash and thoroughly dry the lettuce. Toss into a festive salad bowl and top with the basil leaves. Dress thoroughly but lightly, happily reserving the leftover dressing in the refrigerator for your next salad. Garnish your salad with the croutons, pancetta crisps, and lots of shaved Grana Padano cheese. Elaborately sprinkle with your best salt and lots of pepper. Toss, serve, and share!

A few spoonfuls of reserved bacon or pancetta fat add luxurious richness equally anonymously. It's hard to throw out that kind of flavor, so reserve your bacon fat for moments like this.

Feel free to toss in lots of other flourishes too. Try halving a pint of cherry tomatoes, thinly slicing a red onion, or using baby romaine leaves. If you don't have fresh basil, then fresh parsley leaves are a delicious addition.

FULL-MEAL SALAD

One bowl. One table. One meal. Open your pantry and refrigerator, choose any canned bean, whole grain, nut, dried fruit, seed, and fresh vegetable, then toss with a bright dressing for this nourishing full-meal salad. The possibilities are endless. MAKES ENOUGH FOR 4 MEALS OR 6 SIDES

Begin by choosing and preparing a grain, since it will take the longest and can gently simmer while you compile the rest of the salad. Consult the chart below for your choice, then add the right amount of water and bring to a slow simmer. Once the water is absorbed and your grain is tender, pour it onto a baking sheet to cool for a few minutes before tossing it with the rest of the salad.

Meanwhile, craft the dressing. Fill a large jar with the olive oil, vinegar, mustard, honey, your choice of aromatic spice or herb, salt, and pepper. Shake away until a smooth dressing forms.

Nuts can become stale with time. If you like, refresh their flavor by simply toasting them for a few minutes. Pour and shiver into a single layer on a baking sheet and toast in a 350°F (180°C) oven until they are fragrant and lightly golden brown, 5 minutes or so.

To finish, toss your cooked and cooled grain, drained beans, nuts, dried fruit, seeds, and crunchy fresh vegetables together with the dressing in your favorite salad bowl. Serve and share!

For the salad

1 cup (250 mL) of dried grain, such as barley, bulgur, millet, oats, quinoa, rice, rye berries, or couscous

A 19-ounce (540 mL) can of any cooked beans, chickpeas, or lentils, drained and rinsed

1 cup (250 mL) of whole, chopped, or sliced nuts, such as almonds, pine nuts, walnuts, pistachios, cashews, peanuts, or hazelnuts

1 cup (250 mL) of dried fruit, such as raisins, apricots, figs, dates, apples, or cranberries

1 cup (250 mL) of seeds, such as pumpkin or sunflower

2 carrots, shredded

1 bell pepper, any color, diced, or any other fresh vegetables in the fridge, such as broccoli or cauliflower florets, sliced snow peas, celery, mushrooms, or ripe tomatoes

For the dressing

½ cup (125 mL) of extra-virgin olive oil

¼ cup (60 mL) of any vinegar or fresh lemon juice

¼ cup (60 mL) of grainy or your favorite mustard

2 tablespoons (30 mL) of honey

1 tablespoon (15 mL) of curry powder, ground fennel seed, dried thyme, or dried oregano

¼ teaspoon (1 mL) of salt

Lots of freshly ground pepper

TWIST

The secret to this hearty dish is its vegetarian-friendly combo of a grain and a legume jazzed up with equally nourishing sidekicks. With this written recipe acting as a checklist of sorts, you can create a satisfying meal-in-a-bowl from many different ingredients, whatever you happen to have on hand.

FOR 1 CUP OF DRIED GRAIN

GRAIN	WATER	COOKING TIME
BARLEY	4 CUPS (1 L)	45 MINUTES
BULGUR	2 CUPS (500 ML)	15 MINUTES
MILLET	2½ CUPS (625 ML)	20 MINUTES
OATS, QUICK-COOKING	2 CUPS (500 ML)	5 MINUTES
OATS, OLD-FASHIONED	4 CUPS (1 L)	15 MINUTES
QUINOA	2 CUPS (500 ML)	15 MINUTES
RICE, WHITE	2 CUPS (500 ML)	25 MINUTES
RICE, BROWN, LONG-GRAIN	2½ CUPS (625 ML)	40 MINUTES
RICE, BROWN, SHORT-GRAIN	2 CUPS (500 ML)	45 MINUTES
RICE, WILD	3 CUPS (750 ML)	45 MINUTES
RYE BERRIES	3 CUPS (750 ML)	50 MINUTES
WHEAT BERRIES	3 CUPS (750 ML)	90 MINUTES

STEAKHOUSE SALAD WITH BBQ BLUE CHEESE DRESSING

Every steakhouse features a bold salad tossed with rich, tangy blue cheese and topped with something from the grill. Here's everything you need to craft your own version of this tasty classic. Fire and flame and the rest is up to you! SERVES 4 TO 6

From the grill

A 12-ounce (340 g) New York sirloin, strip, or rib-eye steak (but not flavorless filet mignon)

For the dressing

1 cup (250 mL) of buttermilk

½ cup (125 mL) of your favorite barbecue sauce

¼ cup (60 mL) of red wine vinegar

¼ cup (60 mL) of honey

4 ounces (115 g) of any blue cheese (preferably Gorgonzola), crumbled

½ teaspoon (2 mL) of salt

Lots of freshly ground pepper

For the salad

1 head of iceberg lettuce, chopped

1 head of radicchio, thinly sliced

2 carrots, shredded or sliced

1 red onion, thinly sliced

1 pint (500 mL) of cherry tomatoes, halved

A 3-ounce (85 g) can of crispy onions

Prepare and preheat your barbecue or electric grill to its highest setting. Alternatively, fire up your stove and pan-sear your steak instead. Grill the steak medium-rare. Let rest on a plate while you put the salad together.

Craft the dressing. Fill your food processor or blender with the buttermilk, barbecue sauce, vinegar, honey, blue cheese, salt, and pepper. Blend the works until a smooth dressing forms, just a minute or so.

Fill your favorite festive salad bowl with the lettuce, radicchio, carrots, red onion, and tomatoes. Toss with the dressing and top with the crispy onions and the proceeds of the grill, thinly sliced. Serve and share!

--- TWIST ---

For a quick fix, shred a store-bought rotisserie chicken into this salad. For a BBQ pit version, substitute shredded cabbage for the iceberg lettuce and top the works with pulled pork. Grilled shrimp add a simple seafood theme. And of course bacon in its many delicious forms works as well!

BABY SPINACH & LENTIL SPROUTS

Canada grows the best lentils in the world, and we're the world's biggest exporter of them. It's easy to keep them home, too, because lentils are versatile. Plus they're healthy, hearty, tasty, easy to cook, easy to find, and inexpensive. Just in case you need another reason to cook them, their earthy flavor loves bacon. For maximum lentil love, try sprouting your own—they're seeds and thus easily produce delicious, tender shoots. SERVES 4 TO 6

Begin with the lentil sprouts (see next page). These will take several days, but the results are spectacularly fresh and deliciously healthy. If you don't have the time, no worries, use bean sprouts instead.

Cook the lentils. In a medium saucepan over medium-high heat, bring the lentils, water, and salt to a boil. Reduce the heat to maintain a bare simmer, cover, and continue simmering just until the lentils are tender, about 20 minutes. Strain off any excess water and spread the lentils out on a baking sheet to cool for a few minutes.

Meanwhile, make the dressing. Place your favorite medium saucepan over medium-high heat. Toss in the bacon and a few splashes of water to balance the pan's heat and cook the bacon evenly. Bring to a simmer, stirring frequently with a wooden spoon. As the water simmers, the bacon will begin to cook. Then, as the water evaporates, the bacon will render, releasing its fat. Lastly, it will crisp as the fat left behind heats past the boiling point of water into the flavor zone. Be patient and keep stirring until every piece is evenly crisped, 5 or 6 minutes. Turn off the heat. Using a slotted spoon, remove the bacon bits carefully and set aside, reserving the valuable flavorful bacon drippings. Whisk in the vinegar, honey, and mustard, stirring up all the crispy golden bits in the pan for maximum flavor.

Fill your favorite salad bowl with the cooked lentils and pour every last drop of the bacon dressing all over the works. Stir lovingly. Lightly and gently toss in the onion, spinach, and sprouts just until the salad is evenly coated with the dressing. Top with the crispy bacon bits. Serve and share!

For the lentils

½ cup (125 mL) of dried green, black beluga, or du Puy lentils

2 cups (500 mL) or so of water

¼ teaspoon (1 mL) of sea salt

For the dressing

4 slices of bacon, chopped

3 tablespoons (45 mL) of your favorite vinegar

1 tablespoon (15 mL) of any honey

1 teaspoon (5 mL) of Dijon mustard

For the salad

1 red onion, thinly sliced

5 ounces (140 g) of fresh baby spinach

A few handfuls of fresh lentil sprouts (see next page) or bean sprouts

SPROUTING LENTILS

Lentils are seeds, so with a bit of TLC they're poised to sprout to delicious tenderness and nutritional nirvana. Lentil sprouting is a great way to add a little bit of steam-punk science-experiment fun to your home and grow your own local flavors.

5 or 6 days of your precious time

1 cup (250 mL) of dried green, black beluga, or du Puy lentils

Cut a small piece of mesh screen, about 4 inches (10 cm) square. Pour your lentils into a 1-quart (1 L) jar. Cover the jar's mouth with the screen and tighten on the screw ring (don't use the lid part). This will make it super-easy to rinse and drain your sprouts. Fill the jar with water, drain it through the mesh, and fill it again. Soak the lentils overnight.

The next day, start a twice-daily routine for your lentil babies. Each morning and evening, drain the jar, then fill with fresh water, gently rinse the lentils, and drain them again. Try not to let them sit in water. Rest the jar on its side on a kitchen windowsill. The lentils are starting to grow already, even though you can't see it.

Shortly after the first day, they'll begin to sprout. In three or four days, the sprouts will be about ½ inch (1 cm) long, with small green leaves forming on the ends. They're now at the peak of their nutritional density, tender and full of flavor. Eat them. Or remove the screen, replace the lid on the jar, and store them in the fridge for up to a week.

Lentil sprouts will grow in any climate in just 5 days or so. They don't need soil or sunshine and there's no waste, yet they're packed with nutrients. They're so easy and so much fun to grow that you might forget how versatile they are. A handful of these nutritious treats is perfect for scattering on top of any salad. They're equally delicious crammed into a sandwich and you just might find yourself snacking on 'em straight!

GREEN APPLE SALAD

This salad was inspired by the simplicity of its dressing. When you shake your own simple dressings together, flavor themes emerge and salads like this create themselves. Cider vinegar goes with honey goes with green apple goes with sunflower seeds goes with crispy Cheddar goes with whatever you want it to! SERVES 4

Begin with the cheese toasts. Preheat your oven to 350°F (180°C). Brush one side of the baguette slices with oil. Top with the cheese. Arrange on a baking sheet and bake until the toasts are crispy and the cheese is golden brown and bubbly, about 15 minutes. Set aside to cool while you continue with the salad. Just before serving, break the toasts into smaller pieces.

Next make the dressing. In a small jar, combine the oil, vinegar, honey, mustard, salt, and pepper. Shake vigorously until the mustard takes hold and emulsifies the works into a smooth dressing.

To assemble the salad, fill your favorite festive salad bowl with the salad greens, apple, and seeds. Pour over the dressing and gently toss the works, evenly coating the greens with the dressing. Scatter the toasted cheese baguettes over the salad. Serve and share!

For the cheese toasts

½ of a multigrain baguette, cut on an angle into 12 slices

¼ cup (60 mL) of extra-virgin olive oil

4 ounces (115 g) of your favorite aged Cheddar cheese, shredded

For the dressing

¼ cup (60 mL) of extra-virgin olive oil

2 tablespoons (30 mL) of cider vinegar

1 tablespoon (15 mL) of honey

1 teaspoon (5 mL) of Dijon mustard

¼ teaspoon (1 mL) of salt

Lots of freshly ground pepper

For the salad

5 ounces (140 g) of fresh salad mix

1 Granny Smith apple, cut into matchsticks

½ cup (125 mL) of sunflower seeds

TWIST

Try thinly slicing some prosciutto and gently crisping it in hot olive oil for a savory garnish to this salad.

This salad is a derivative of the basic salad on page 4. It shows how a flavor theme can accelerate your ideas as you freestyle your own food.

WARM KALE, WHITE BEAN & CRANBERRY SALAD

Few things in the vegetable repertoire are healthier than dark green kale. It's packed with flavor and a laundry list of minerals and micronutrients. Its leaves are easy to cook and its hearty flavor is easy to get along with. Kale and white beans anchor this warm salad side dish where they're brightened with sharp cranberries and crunchy rye croutons. **SERVES 4 TO 6**

For the croutons

4 thick slices of rye bread, cubed or torn

2 tablespoons (30 mL) of water

2 tablespoons (30 mL) of olive oil

For the dressing

¼ cup (60 mL) of red wine vinegar

¼ cup (60 mL) of honey

2 tablespoons (30 mL) of your best extra-virgin olive oil

1 tablespoon (15 mL) of Dijon mustard

¼ teaspoon (1 mL) of salt

For the salad

1 bunch of dark green kale

1 cup (250 mL) of dried cranberries

A 19-ounce (540 mL) can of white kidney beans, drained and rinsed

1 cup (250 mL) or so of whole, slivered, or sliced almonds

Begin with the croutons. Preheat your oven to 350°F (180°C) and turn on your convection fan if you have one. Put the bread cubes in a large bowl, sprinkle them with water, then toss with the olive oil. Scatter evenly on a baking sheet and bake until crispy and crunchy, 15 to 20 minutes. The water helps the croutons stay chewy on the inside while the oil helps them crisp on the outside.

Mix the dressing. In a jar, combine the vinegar, honey, olive oil, mustard, and salt. Shake vigorously until the mustard kicks in and a smooth dressing forms.

Prepare the kale. Cut the stalky stems away from the leaves. Stack the leaves, roll tightly, and cut into ½-inch (1 cm) slices.

Fit a large saucepan with a steamer basket. Fill the pot with a few inches of water and bring to a vigorous boil. Sprinkle the cranberries in the steamer basket and cover with the kale. Cover and steam until the kale softens, shrinks, and transforms from dark green to brighter green, about 3 minutes.

To serve, toss the kale, cranberries, beans, almonds, and croutons with the dressing. Serve and share!

TWIST

This dish is a sophisticated way to encourage kale consumption by elevating it to the echelon of fancy salad. Once you see how easy it is to steam kale tender, you'll be ready to pile some bright green goodness onto any dinner plate!

MEDITERRANEAN CHICKPEA, TOMATO & CUCUMBER SALAD

With a can of chickpeas in hand, a handful of flavorful dried tomatoes, and a crunchy cucumber, you're just a few twists and turns away from this simple, satisfying salad. Toss together a tangy-sweet tomato dressing and you'll feel the bright Mediterranean in this dish. **SERVES 4 TO 6**

Begin with the dressing. Fill your food processor or blender with the dried tomatoes, oil, vinegar, oregano, mustard, and salt. Process the works until a smooth dressing forms, 30 seconds or so.

In your favorite salad bowl, toss the chickpeas, cucumber, cherry tomatoes, and green onions together with the dressing. Garnish with the parsley leaves. Serve and share!

TWIST

Handfuls of fresh herb leaves are excellent last-second additions to most salads. Lighter herbs such as dill, mint, cilantro, and the parsleys work best. Heavier herbs, like rosemary, sage, and oregano, are a bit too strong. Try adding handfuls of fresh basil leaves for a spectacular flavor revelation!

For the dressing

½ cup (125 mL) of best quality dried tomatoes (preferably oil packed)

½ cup (125 mL) of your very best extra-virgin olive oil

¼ cup (60 mL) of red wine vinegar

1 tablespoon (15 mL) of dried oregano

1 tablespoon (15 mL) of Dijon or other mustard

¼ teaspoon (1 mL) of salt

For the salad

A 19-ounce (540 mL) can of chickpeas, drained and rinsed

1 English cucumber, cut in 4 long pieces, then in 1-inch (2.5 cm) chunks

1 pint (500 mL) of cherry tomatoes, quartered

A few thinly sliced green onions

A few handfuls of fresh parsley leaves

ARUGULA SALAD WITH GOAT CHEESE & PEARS

Walnut-crusted baked goat cheese, pan-roasted pears, sharp nutty arugula, sweet-sour dressing—it's got everything! Bonus: you can prep it all in advance and shine at the last minute. SERVES 6

For the dressing

2 tablespoons (30 mL) of walnut oil

2 tablespoons (30 mL) of cider vinegar

2 tablespoons (30 mL) of your favorite honey

1 tablespoon (15 mL) of Dijon mustard

½ teaspoon (2 mL) of salt

Lots of freshly ground pepper

For the goat cheese

½ cup (125 mL) of all-purpose flour

2 eggs

½ cup (125 mL) of walnuts

¼ cup (60 mL) of dry bread crumbs

A 10-ounce (280 g) log of goat cheese, sliced in 6 even pucks

For the salad

3 pears (preferably Anjou)

A splash of olive oil

½ cup (125 mL) of walnuts

6 large handfuls of arugula

TWIST

Try coating the goat cheese with different nuts, such as almonds, pecans, cashews, hazelnuts, macadamias, or even wasabi peas. Each nut will bring a different flavor to the party.

Preheat your oven to 400°F (200°C). Line a small baking sheet with parchment paper.

Begin with the dressing. Pour the walnut oil, cider vinegar, honey, mustard, salt, and pepper into a jar. Shake vigorously for a few moments until a smooth dressing forms. Set aside.

Prepare the goat cheese. Line up 3 shallow bowls. Put the flour in the first bowl. Whisk the eggs together in the second bowl. Put the walnuts and bread crumbs into your food processor and blend until they resemble a coarse powder, just 30 seconds or so. Transfer to the third bowl.

To avoid messy hands, use one hand to handle the cheese pucks while they're dry and the other while they're wet. Dip and roll each goat cheese piece first in the flour, shaking off any excess. Then dip into the eggs, again shaking off the excess. Finally dip into the walnut mixture, coating thoroughly. The flour allows for maximum egg coating and thus maximum walnut crusting as well. Place on the baking sheet and set aside.

Prepare the pears. Heat your favorite heavy skillet over medium-high heat. Cut the pears in half from top to bottom straight through the core, then use either a spoon or a melon-baller to scoop out the core and seeds. Turn off the pan's heat, then add a splash of olive oil to the pan, enough to coat the bottom with a thin film. Carefully place the pears cut side down, then put the hot pan in the oven along with the goat cheese.

Bake until the pears are golden brown and the goat cheese is also deliciously browned, 15 minutes or so. Toast the remaining ½ cup (125 mL) of walnuts in the oven, about 3 minutes.

To serve, in a large bowl, toss together the arugula, toasted walnuts, and dressing. Place a large handful in each individual salad bowl. Top with a warm pear half and one portion of crusted goat cheese.

TOMATO BASIL QUINOA SALAD

Quinoa isn't a true grain; it's actually more closely related to beets and spinach, which may explain its incredible nutritional profile. It is high in all eight essential amino acids as well as calcium, phosphorus, and iron. Bottom line? Quinoa is so healthy and so easy to cook that you can't afford not to have it on your table! **SERVES 4 TO 6**

Begin with the quinoa. Rinse it well and let it drain for a few minutes. Heat the vegetable oil in your favorite medium saucepan over medium-high heat. Toss the quinoa into the pan. Toast the quinoa, gently stirring occasionally, until golden brown and aromatic, about 5 minutes. Add the water, salt, and pepper. Lower the heat, cover, and simmer until the water is absorbed and the quinoa is tender, 15 minutes or so. Cool to room temperature while you prepare the rest of the salad.

In a festive salad bowl, combine the cherry tomatoes, basil leaves, and red onion. Craft the dressing by pouring the vinegar, oil, honey, and mustard into a small jar and shake, shake, shaking! Pour the dressing over the salad, then add the cooled quinoa. Lightly toss everything together. Serve and share!

For the quinoa

1 cup (250 mL) of quinoa

2 tablespoons (30 mL) of vegetable oil

2 cups (500 mL) of water

½ teaspoon (2 mL) of salt

Lots of freshly ground pepper

For the salad

2 pints (1 L) of cherry tomatoes, halved

Leaves from 2 or 3 bunches of fresh basil

1 red onion, thinly sliced

For the dressing

¼ cup (60 mL) of balsamic vinegar

¼ cup (60 mL) of your best extra-virgin olive oil

2 tablespoons (30 mL) of honey

1 tablespoon (15 mL) of Dijon mustard

-------------------- TWIST --------------------

Quinoa is so nutritious and easy to cook that it's a great ingredient for stirring into just about any salad, soup, or stew. With this basic cooking method, you're ready for a last-minute addition to any meal.

SWEET POTATO PICNIC SALAD

A classic potato salad is a regular guest at any picnic, but it's always fun to invite a few new flavors along too. Brighten things up by replacing plain white potatoes with sweet potatoes. Throw in a sweet-and-sour honey-mustard dressing and you're guaranteed a lifetime picnic invitation! SERVES 4 TO 6

For the salad

2 large or 3 smaller sweet potatoes (unpeeled)

2 tablespoons (30 mL) of olive oil

2 green onions, chopped

2 ribs of celery, diced

A handful or so of fresh parsley leaves

½ cup (125 mL) of chopped pecans

½ cup (125 mL) of dried cranberries

For the dressing

2 tablespoons (30 mL) of red wine vinegar

2 tablespoons (30 mL) of Dijon mustard

1 tablespoon (15 mL) of mayonnaise

1 tablespoon (15 mL) of honey

1 teaspoon (5 mL) of salt

A few splashes of your favorite hot sauce

Preheat your oven to 350°F (180°C) and turn on your convection fan if you have one.

Begin with the sweet potatoes. Cut them in half lengthwise, then into even cubes. Place them in a festive salad bowl, add the olive oil, and toss the works together. Spread in an even layer on a baking sheet. Roast the potatoes until they're golden brown and crispy delicious, 30 minutes or so.

Wipe out the salad bowl with a paper towel, then add the vinegar, mustard, mayonnaise, honey, salt, and hot sauce. Whisk the dressing until smooth. Toss in the green onions, celery, parsley, pecans, and cranberries. Add the potatoes and give the works a thorough last-second toss. Serve and share!

TWIST

You don't *have* to approach cooking creatively, but you can, and doing so can often get you out of a rut. One of the best ways to start is to simply swap equivalent ingredients, like sweet potatoes for white potatoes.

GREEN ON
CELERY
PARSLEY
PECANS
CRAN BE
HONEY

SWEET-AND-SOUR OVERNIGHT FENNEL SLAW

Slaws are usually anchored by shredded cabbage, but really any shredded hearty vegetable will do. Especially fennel. This slaw shows off the surprisingly sweet licorice flavor of my favorite vegetable. It's a great way to add fresh fennel to your table. SERVES 4

Begin with the dressing. Fill a small jar with the lemon zest and juice, coriander seeds, olive oil, honey, mustard, and salt. Shake the works vigorously until the emulsifying lecithin within the mustard works its magic and a smooth dressing forms.

Prepare the salad. Cut off and discard the long green stalks from the top of the fennel bulb, saving any feathery fronds if you wish to toss them in the salad at the end. To grate by hand, cut the bulb in half lengthwise but leave the woody core in place. This will help the layers of the fennel hold together while you grate it. Shred through the large holes of a box grater until you reach the woody core, which can be discarded or enjoyed as a quick snack. Alternatively, trim out the woody core and grate the fennel in a food processor.

In a large bowl, toss together the grated fennel, carrots, and red onion. Splash in the dressing and toss the works again, evenly distributing the bright flavors and crisp vegetables. You can serve and share this slaw immediately, but it will be even better the next day. The overnight rest will give the flavors time to meld and the textures time to soften.

For the dressing
The zest and juice of 1 lemon

2 heaping tablespoons (35 mL) of coriander seeds

2 tablespoons (30 mL) of extra-virgin olive oil

1 tablespoon (15 mL) of your favorite honey

1 tablespoon (15 mL) of Dijon mustard

¼ teaspoon (1 mL) of salt

For the salad
1 fennel bulb

2 carrots, grated

1 small red onion, thinly sliced

TWIST

Slaws are very informal affairs and are thus ripe for creative picking. Choose a favorite flavor or two and create your own signature slaw. Raw fennel is also ripe for creative license. It can brighten any salad or vegetable dish with its fresh licorice flavor.

CHICKEN

SIMPLE ROASTED CHICKEN

There are many ways to cook a chicken. The best methods add flavor, and this one includes fun. You can confidently perch a chicken on a thick bed of flavorful vegetables and roast the works knowing that a humble but hearty meal awaits. With no regard for classic propriety, you can then shred the roasted bird over the tender veggies, capturing all the goodness in a spontaneous pan stew—and neatly ducking any sharp-knife angst. You'll even end up with next-day broth! SERVES 4 TO 6, EVEN 8 IN A PINCH

A fresh roasting chicken
(4 to 5 pounds/1.8 to 2.25 kg)

With roasted tomatoes and oregano

2 or 3 onions, peeled and
cut in 8 wedges

8 plum tomatoes, halved

1 tablespoon (15 mL) of
dried oregano

½ teaspoon (2 mL) of salt

Lots of freshly ground pepper

1 head of garlic, halved

Leaves from 1 bunch of fresh
oregano or basil, chopped

**With cinnamon apples and
sweet potatoes**

3 sweet potatoes (unpeeled), cubed

3 apples, cored and cut in 8 wedges

3 onions, peeled and cut in 8 wedges

2 teaspoons (10 mL) of cinnamon

½ teaspoon (2 mL) of salt

Lots of freshly ground pepper

1 cup (250 mL) of apple cider,
apple juice, or your favorite wine

2 or 3 green onions, thinly sliced

Preheat your oven to 400°F (200°C) and turn on your convection fan if you have one.

Get out a large, heavy roasting pan, large enough to hold the chicken. Choose your flavor theme—or create your own bed of flavors. Put your chosen vegetables with their seasonings (but not the fresh herbs or the green onions) in the pan. You can follow the amounts given here or fill the pan with as much flavor as you like, knowing that as the chicken roasts, its juices will mingle with the veggies, the contents magically transforming into a tasty dinner. Toss the works together, then evenly distribute them in the pan.

Season the chicken inside and out with salt and pepper and rest it breast side up on top of the vegetable mixture. If you chose the cinnamon apple option, now is the time to pour in the cider. Place the chicken in the oven and lower the temperature to 350°F (180°C).

The bird will reliably take about 20 minutes per pound. It does not require basting. After an hour or so take the bird's temperature in the thickest part of the thigh. When it reaches 180°F (85°C) you'll know it's perfectly done, juicy and delicious. The veggies should be nicely done too, but sometimes they need a little more time. It's OK for them to roast a bit longer, even brown deliciously, as the chicken cooks a bit more and you ready the rest of the meal.

Once you pull the chicken from the oven you can serve it immediately—you don't need to wait for the meat to rest since any juices that leak during carving will be mixed with the pan stew. Using 2 sets of tongs, and with the bird still in the pan, slice and pull the meat from the bones. Transfer the bones to a saucepan for simmering into rich broth for another meal. Gently mix the crispy skin and succulent meat with the roasted vegetables. Sprinkle with your fresh herbs or green onions at the last second, thus preserving their fresh flavor and fragrance. And feel free to enjoy the spoils that accrue to the cook, the tender, juicy, crispy bits. Serve from the pan!

TWIST

A perfect roast chicken relies on an accurate meat thermometer, a simple investment that always pays dividends. Don't assume the one you have is accurate, either. Check it by holding the last inch or so of the tip in boiling water—it should read 212°F (100°C). Calibrate according to the manufacturer's instructions.

See photo on the next page

PAN-RUSHED CHICKEN FLAVORS

Pan-rushing is one of many line-cook moves we chefs pick up early on in our illustrious careers. It's a common trick in the trenches of fine dining that respects the food yet maximizes precious resources. It involves an initial high-heat sear of a chicken breast, pork chop, or steak followed by a slow-heat finish while simultaneously crafting the matching sauce. Three simple steps: sear, sauce, and simmer. Brilliant! What's on the menu? It's your choice! SERVES 4 TO 6

For the chicken
4 boneless, skinless chicken breasts

2 tablespoons (30 mL) of vegetable oil

For a fragrant Indian curry
1 onion, diced

4 garlic cloves, minced

2 tablespoons (30 mL) of curry powder

¼ teaspoon (1 mL) of salt

½ cup (125 mL) of Major Grey chutney or orange marmalade

A 19-ounce (540 mL) can of chickpeas, drained and rinsed

A 19-ounce (540 mL) can of diced tomatoes

1 bunch of fresh cilantro

For the Mediterranean special-of-the-day
1 onion, diced

4 garlic cloves, minced

1 tablespoon (15 mL) of dried oregano

¼ teaspoon (1 mL) of salt

Lots of freshly ground pepper

A 19-ounce (540 mL) can of diced tomatoes

1 cup (250 mL) of pitted great olives, kalamata or otherwise

½ cup (125 mL) of your favorite red wine

4 handfuls of fresh baby spinach

Leaves from 1 bunch of fresh basil, or flat-leaf parsley sprigs, or both

Sear the chicken breasts. Match your favorite large, heavy skillet with a tight-fitting lid and medium-high heat. Splash in enough vegetable oil to thinly coat the bottom of the pan. As soon as you see a wisp of smoke, carefully commit the chicken breasts to the searing-hot pan. Adjust the heat if needed, trying to keep the works sizzling without smoking. The goal here is not to fully cook the meat but just to add lots of brown flavor while the pan temperature is high. Sear each side of the chicken until golden brown, 4 or 5 minutes each side. Transfer the chicken to a plate.

CURRIED CHICKEN Return the pan to medium heat and add the onion, garlic, curry powder, and salt. Sauté until soft and fragrant, a minute or two of brightening, then stir in the chutney, chickpeas, and tomatoes.

MEDITERRANEAN CHICKEN Return the pan to medium heat and add the onion, garlic, oregano, salt, and pepper. Sauté for a minute or two, softening textures and strengthening flavors. Add the tomatoes, olives, and wine.

SOUTHWESTERN CHICKEN Return the pan to medium heat and add the bell pepper, onion, garlic, chili powder, and salt. Sauté for a minute or two, softening textures and strengthening flavors. Add the tomatoes and beans.

In each case, reduce the heat to a slow, steady simmer. Return the chicken breasts and any juices to the pan, nestling them into the flavorful sauce. Cover tightly and simmer until the chicken is cooked through, another 5 to 10 minutes. Turn the chicken over once during cooking to allow the flavors to fully permeate the meat from all sides.

Serve the curried chicken over basmati rice, topped with handfuls of cilantro leaves and tender stems.

Serve the Mediterranean chicken over baby spinach, sprinkled with fresh herb leaves.

Serve the southwestern chicken over brown rice, topped with cilantro leaves and lime wedges.

For spicy southwestern flavors

1 red bell pepper, chopped

1 onion, diced

4 garlic cloves, minced

1 tablespoon (15 mL) of chili powder

¼ teaspoon (1 mL) of salt

A 19-ounce (540 mL) can of diced tomatoes

A 19-ounce (540 mL) can of black or red beans, drained and rinsed

Leaves from 1 bunch of fresh cilantro

2 limes, cut into wedges

- - - - - - - - - - - - - - **TWIST** - - - - - - - - - - - - - -

If you enjoy the inherent creativity of cooking and like trying out new freestyle ideas, then pan-rushing a round of chicken breasts is for you. My versions are full of reliable flavor, but feel free to create your own. Find a flavor theme for your pan. Choose aromatic ingredients and liquids to fill it. You'll soon be able to write your own cookbook filled with your own flavors!

See photo on the next page

INDIAN CURRY

SOUTHWESTERN

MEDITERRANEAN

OLIVE FETA CRUSTED CHICKEN

Of the many ways to add flavor to a chicken breast, crusting is one of the tastiest, especially when feta cheese and black olives are in the mix. SERVES 4

Preheat your oven to 375°F (190°C) and turn on your convection fan if you have one.

Sear the chicken breasts before crusting them. Heat your favorite large, heavy skillet over medium-high heat. Splash in enough vegetable oil to thinly coat the bottom of the pan. As soon as you see a wisp of smoke, carefully commit the chicken breasts to the searing-hot pan. Adjust the heat if needed, trying to keep the works sizzling without smoking. The goal here is not to fully cook the meat but just to add lots of brown flavor while the pan temperature is high. Sear each side of the chicken until golden brown, 4 or 5 minutes each side. Transfer the seared chicken to a baking dish.

Prepare the feta crust by piling the bread crumbs, olive oil, oregano, and feta into your food processor. Pulse just until wet crumbs form and everything is mixed well. Add the kalamata olives and pulse just a few more times, chopping the olives without puréeing them and turning the mixture purple-black. Top each chicken breast with some of the crust, patting it into an even layer of flavor.

Bake the chicken breasts, finishing their interior cooking and lightly browning their new crust, for 20 minutes or so, until they register an internal temperature of 165°F (75°C). Serve and share!

For the chicken

4 boneless, skinless chicken breasts

2 tablespoons (30 mL) of vegetable oil

For the crust

½ cup (125 mL) of dry bread crumbs

¼ cup (60 mL) of your very best extra-virgin olive oil

1 heaping tablespoon (18 mL) of dried oregano

4 ounces (115 g) of feta cheese, crumbled

½ cup (125 mL) or so of pitted kalamata olives

TWIST

You can easily freestyle this recipe by replacing an ingredient in the base version with an equivalent amount of a similar ingredient. Pick a flavor theme and impress yourself.

BREAD CRUMBS: various fresh or dried; even a variety of whole-grain breakfast cereals add interesting textures

OIL: any olive oil, fragrant walnut oil, melted butter

AROMATIC HERBS: your choice, fresh or dried

CHEESES: Boursin, Cheddar, Brie, Parmesan, Stilton

OLIVES: any olives, or dried tomatoes, nuts, or other condiments

---

MOROCCAN BRAISED CHICKEN WITH CARROT MINT COUSCOUS

Chicken is easily cooked and just as easily flavored. Its Moroccan street cred goes up with ras el hanout—literally "best of the shop"—a custom blend of the best spices in the shop by the bargaining merchant. Just like the blends I tasted in the casbahs and souks of Marrakesh.
SERVES 4 TO 6

For the chicken

A splash of vegetable oil

6 chicken thighs complete with skin and bones

1 carrot, chopped

2 onions, chopped

4 garlic cloves, sliced

1 tablespoon (15 mL) of ras el hanout

½ cup (125 mL) of pistachios

½ cup (125 mL) of kalamata olives

½ cup (125 mL) of halved dried figs

½ cup (125 mL) of orange marmalade

1 cup (250 mL) of orange juice

The zest and juice of 1 lemon

½ teaspoon (2 mL) of salt

For the carrot mint couscous

1½ cups (375 mL) of water

2 tablespoons (30 mL) of olive oil

1 teaspoon (5 mL) of any vinegar

1 carrot, shredded

Leaves from 1 bunch of fresh mint, sliced

1 cup (250 mL) of couscous

½ teaspoon (2 mL) of salt

Match your favorite heavy skillet with a tight-fitting lid and medium-high heat. Splash and swirl in enough vegetable oil to thinly coat the bottom of the pan. Add the chicken thighs and sear the first side until golden brown and crusty, 4 to 5 minutes. Flip and sear the second side until it's equally golden brown. The goal here is not to fully cook the meat but just to add lots of brown flavor while the pan temperature is high. Reduce the heat to medium and transfer the chicken to a plate.

Add the carrot, onions, and garlic to the pan. Sauté for a minute or two, heating through. Sprinkle in the ras el hanout and sauté for a minute or so more, softening textures and brightening spice flavors. Stir in the pistachios, olives, figs, marmalade, orange juice, lemon zest and juice, and salt. Bring the works to a slow, steady simmer. Return the chicken and any juices to the pan, cover tightly, lower the heat further, and continue to gently simmer until the thighs reach an internal temperature of 165°F (75°C), about 15 minutes.

While the chicken is simmering, prepare the couscous. In a small pot, bring the water, olive oil, and vinegar to a steady simmer, stirring along the way. Turn off the heat. Stir in the carrot, mint, couscous, and salt, then immediately cover with a tight-fitting lid. Let rest for at least 5 minutes—long enough for the chicken to catch up! Dinner is ready to eat now, but if you have time for maximum tenderness, adjust your heat to the lowest setting and carry on simmering the chicken for another 45 minutes or so.

> **TWIST**
>
> In the universal spirit of spice blending you can easily craft your own custom blend of ras el hanout inspired by Moroccan spice shops. Remember all the "c" spices: cardamom, cloves, cinnamon, coriander, chili powder, cumin, caraway, and even curry. I like to add a bit of fennel seed and dried ginger too. You'll be amazed how fragrant, delicious, and simple it can be to blend your own in a jar.

CARIBBEAN BRAISED CHICKEN WITH SWEET POTATO MASH

Nothing beats a festive pan full of Caribbean flavors. Pan-seared chicken thighs simmered till tender with pineapple juice, dark rum, juicy mangoes, island spices, and habanero chili, served alongside sweet potatoes mashed with coconut. SERVES 4 TO 6

Begin with the chicken. Match your favorite large, heavy skillet with a tight-fitting lid and medium-high heat. Splash in enough vegetable oil to thinly coat the bottom of the pan. Add the chicken thighs and sear the first side until golden brown and crusty, 4 to 5 minutes. Flip and sear the second side until it's equally golden brown. The goal here is not to fully cook the meat but just to add lots of brown flavor while the pan temperature is high. Reduce the heat to medium and transfer the chicken to a plate.

Add the onion, garlic, red pepper, habanero chili, ginger, cinnamon, allspice, and salt to the pan. Sauté for a minute or two, heating through, softening textures, and brightening spice flavors. Add the pineapple juice and rum. Bring to a slow, steady simmer. Return the chicken and any juices to the pan, nestling the chicken into the sauce. Add one last layer of flavor with the mango slices arranged in a spoke pattern on top. Cover tightly, lower the heat further, and continue gently simmering until the thighs reach an internal temperature of 165°F (75°C), about 15 minutes.

While the chicken simmers, make the sweet potato mash. Combine the coconut milk, nutmeg, vanilla, and salt in a medium saucepan. Stir in the sweet potatoes and bring to a slow, steady simmer over medium heat. Simmer, stirring frequently, until the sweet potatoes soften, 20 minutes or so. Turn off the heat, mash the works, and set aside, covered. Just before serving, stir in the green onions.

Spoon the fragrant, tender chicken over mounds of sweet potato mash and sprinkle cilantro leaves all over the works.

For the chicken

A splash of vegetable oil

6 boneless, skinless chicken thighs

1 red onion, thinly sliced

Cloves from 1 head of garlic, chopped

2 red bell peppers, chopped

1 habanero chili, halved, seeded, and finely chopped

A 1-inch (2.5 cm) knob of frozen ginger, grated

1 teaspoon (5 mL) of cinnamon

1 teaspoon (5 mL) of ground allspice

½ teaspoon (2 mL) of salt

2 cups (500 mL) of pineapple juice

¼ cup (60 mL) of dark rum

2 ripe mangoes, peeled and sliced

A few handfuls of fresh cilantro leaves

For the sweet potato mash

A 14-ounce (400 mL) can of coconut milk

1 whole nutmeg, grated (about 2 teaspoons/10 mL)

1 tablespoon (15 mL) of vanilla extract

A pinch of salt

2 large or 3 or 4 medium sweet potatoes (unpeeled), cut in small chunks

2 green onions, chopped

TWIST

This dish is best when it follows an island-inspired cocktail. Challenge your next dinner party to create their own libation using some of the ingredients in the main dish. Have extra of everything on hand!

THAI CHICKEN BROTH WITH SWEET POTATO AND CILANTRO BEAN SPROUT SALAD

Thai food is memorable for many things: bright colors and flavors, contrasting tastes, intriguing textures, and especially mysterious, tantalizing aromas. All are easily stirred into these bowls of delicious goodness. SERVES 4 TO 6

For the chicken broth

2 tablespoons (30 mL) of vegetable oil

2 onions, diced

4 garlic cloves, minced

A few inches (5 cm or so) of fresh ginger, peeled and thinly sliced

1 tablespoon (15 mL) of your favorite Thai curry paste (yellow, green, or red)

2 sweet potatoes (unpeeled), cubed

6 chicken thighs, bone-in but skin gone, who knows where

3 or 4 lime leaves

A 19-ounce (540 mL) can of diced tomatoes

A 14-ounce (400 mL) can of coconut milk

2 tablespoons (30 mL) of fish sauce

For the salad

10 ounces (280 g) of fresh baby spinach

1 bunch of fresh cilantro

4 large handfuls of bean sprouts

The zest and juice of 1 lime

Begin with the chicken broth. Place a large stockpot over medium-high heat. Splash in the oil, then sauté the onions, garlic, and ginger until they're lightly softened and fragrant, 2 or 3 minutes. Thoroughly stir in the curry paste, awakening lingering flavors for a few moments, before adding the sweet potatoes, chicken thighs, lime leaves, diced tomatoes, and coconut milk. Bring the works to a vigorous simmer, then reduce the heat to a bare simmer and cook, uncovered, for 1 hour or until the chicken is tender enough to fall away from the bones. Get rid of the bones, and stir in the fish sauce. Remove from the heat.

Divide the spinach among 4 or 6 small festive bowls. Toss together the cilantro, bean sprouts, and lime zest and juice. Ladle the fragrant chicken broth over the spinach and top with the cilantro bean sprout salad. Serve and share!

TWIST

There are three readily available Thai spice pastes, each distinctively flavored, each with a different level of spiciness. Yellow is the mildest and derives its flavors solely from fragrant spices, not chili peppers. Green curry paste contains the same spices but is sharpened by the heat of green chilies. Red curry paste is loaded with fully ripened red chili peppers and explosive heat. Take your table to the spicy flavor edge!

SOUTHWESTERN FRIED CHICKEN

Fried chicken is one of the world's great comfort foods, and it's easy to do really well. It's great deliciously crispy and plain but even better with lots of spices in the crust. Your best choice for high-temp frying, precision crisping, and flavor is good old-fashioned lard. SERVES 6

Cut your chicken into 10 pieces: 2 thighs, 2 drumsticks, 2 wings, and 4 breast pieces (or ask your butcher to do it for you, or purchase separate pieces). In a large resealable plastic bag, shake together the brown sugar, chili powder, smoked paprika, cumin, and salt. Add the chicken pieces and shake enthusiastically until they're well coated with the spice rub. Pour in the buttermilk, seal the bag tightly, massage evenly, and let marinate in the fridge. A minimum of 2 hours is best, and overnight is even better.

When you're ready to forge forward, slightly open one end of the seal and drain the marinade. Transfer the marinated chicken to a dry large resealable plastic bag. Add the flour and shake, shake, shake until the chicken pieces are evenly coated. Arrange the chicken pieces on a baking sheet and let dry for 15 minutes or so before frying.

Melt the lard in your favorite high-sided skillet or large pot over medium-high heat. Adjust the heat until a deep-fat thermometer reads 375°F (190°C).

Carefully add a single layer of chicken pieces to the hot fat, being careful not to crowd the pan. Cook one side until it's golden brown and crispy, 10 minutes or so, then flip and give the same treatment to the other side. The fat will cool slightly and you may need to crank the heat to keep it close to 375°F (190°C). Carefully remove the chicken and drain on paper towels. Return the fat to 375°F and repeat with the remaining chicken pieces. Serve and share!

1 whole fryer chicken
¼ cup (60 mL) of brown sugar
¼ cup (60 mL) or so of chili powder
2 tablespoons (30 mL) of smoked paprika
1 tablespoon (15 mL) of ground cumin
1 tablespoon (15 mL) of salt
2 cups (500 mL) of buttermilk
2 heaping cups (550 mL) of all-purpose flour
1 pound (450 g) of lard

TWIST

Part of the grand southern tradition of fried chicken is to boast that your signature version contains the best and most essential blend of agreeable herbs and spices. In that vein, feel free to craft your own custom blend of flavors.

To add even more spice to the chicken, add to the flour some of the same spices that are in the rub.

CRISPY CRUSTY CHICKEN STRIPS WITH GLOBAL DIPS

There's just something about crispy, crusty chicken strips that little hands love and love to dip into creamy flavors. Choose one of the dips or all of them, because it ain't junk food when you make it yourself! SERVES 4

For the crispy crusty chicken strips

2 boneless, skinless chicken breasts

1 cup (250 mL) of all-purpose flour

1 teaspoon (5 mL) of salt

Lots of freshly ground pepper

1 teaspoon of spice to match your dip choice: chili powder, curry powder, or five spice

4 eggs

1 cup (250 mL) of panko bread crumbs, plain dry bread crumbs, or even dried potato flakes

For the southwestern dip

½ cup (125 mL) of sour cream

½ cup (125 mL) of your favorite salsa

1 teaspoon (5 mL) of ground cumin

A splash of your favorite hot sauce

The juice of ½ lime

For the Indian dip

½ cup (125 mL) of plain yogurt

1 tablespoon (15 mL) of mango chutney

1 teaspoon (5 mL) of curry powder

For the Asian dip

¼ cup (60 mL) of sour cream

1 tablespoon (15 mL) of soy sauce

1 teaspoon (5 mL) of honey

1-inch (2.5 cm) piece of fresh ginger, peeled and grated

Juice of ½ lime

A dash or two of sesame oil

Preheat your oven to 375°F (190°C) and turn on your convection fan if you have one. Line a baking sheet with parchment paper.

Slice each of the chicken breasts into 6 long strips. Get out 3 shallow bowls. In the first bowl, stir together the flour, salt, pepper, and chosen spice. Lightly whisk the eggs together in the second bowl. Spread the bread crumbs in the third bowl.

To avoid messy hands, use one hand to handle the chicken strips while they're dry and the other while they're wet. Dip and roll the chicken slices first in the flour, shaking off any excess. Then dip them into the eggs, again shaking off the excess. Finally, dip them in the bread crumbs, coating thoroughly. The flour allows for maximum egg coating and thus maximum crumb crusting as well. Arrange the chicken strips on the baking sheet and bake until crispy and golden brown, 15 to 20 minutes.

Meanwhile, in a small festive bowl, stir together the ingredients of your chosen dip. Serve and share the chicken strips with the dip-of-the-day!

TWIST

The flavor and texture of chicken is universally bland and neutral, so you can reliably add the flavor theme of your choice to both the crust and the dip.

SPICE ROAST CHICKEN WINGS

Chicken wings are one of the all-time great comfort foods, and you don't need a restaurant-grade deep-fryer to enjoy them at their best. With this deceptively simple method it's just plain easy to toss together a batch and roast them to perfection. Guaranteed deliciously crispy, aromatic, and tender results. **SERVES 2 TO 4, EASILY DOUBLED**

Preheat your oven to 350°F (180°C) and turn on your convection oven if you have one.

Whisk together the cornstarch, sugar, chosen seasoning, salt, and pepper in a large bowl. Add the chicken wings and toss until they're evenly coated. Neatly arrange the wings on a baking sheet.

Bake the wings until they're crispy brown on the outside yet still juicy on the inside, about 1 hour. Serve and share!

¼ cup (60 mL) of cornstarch

2 tablespoons (30 mL) of sugar

1 heaping tablespoon (18 mL) or so of dried thyme, curry or chili powder, or your favorite dried herb or spice

2 teaspoons (10 mL) of salt

2 teaspoons (10 mL) of freshly ground pepper

12 whole chicken wings, tips attached

TWIST

Chicken wings get crispy and deliciously juicy and tender with this basic cooking method. Experiment by adding distinctive aromatic flavors to the works. Sage, rosemary, savory, and oregano are excellent herb choices, while cumin and Old Bay are great spices. But you may discover that you just can't beat plain salt and pepper!

FISH WINGS

These wings come with a secret. Not only are they addictively delicious but their savory flavor source is deceptively mysterious. Everyone will love the aromatic fermented fish flavors—until you mention where they come from. Or not. By the time the table finds out there's fish sauce involved, there won't be any turning back anyway. Just a pile of wing bones and shouts for more. MAKES 24 WHOLE WINGS, ENOUGH FOR A PARTY

½ cup (125 mL) of brown sugar

½ cup (125 mL) of ketchup

¼ cup (60 mL) of fish sauce

¼ cup (60 mL) or so of sambal oelek or your favorite chili-garlic sauce

¼ cup (60 mL) or so of grated frozen ginger

24 whole chicken wings (or 48 chicken wing sections, a mixture of drums and flats)

In a large bowl, whisk together the brown sugar, ketchup, fish sauce, sambal, and ginger. Add the chicken wings and toss to coat well. Marinate, covered and refrigerated, overnight if possible.

Preheat your oven to 350°F (180°C) and turn on your convection fan if you have one. Line a baking sheet with parchment paper for speedy cleanup.

Arrange the flavored wings on the baking sheet, reserving the leftover sauce. Bake the wings until they're tender and juicy, 45 minutes or so.

Meanwhile, pour the remaining sauce into a pot over medium heat. Stirring frequently, heat the works until it's bubbling. Continue cooking until the sauce thickens noticeably, becoming a glaze, about 5 minutes. Turn off the heat. When the wings are done, immediately transfer them to a large bowl and toss them with the hot, sticky sauce. Serve, share, and get ready to lick your fingers!

> **TWIST**
>
> This basic saucing method works well for many soupy sweet marinades and wing sauces. The liquid is not safe after marinating raw poultry, so it's either discarded or boiled and safely returned to the wings later.

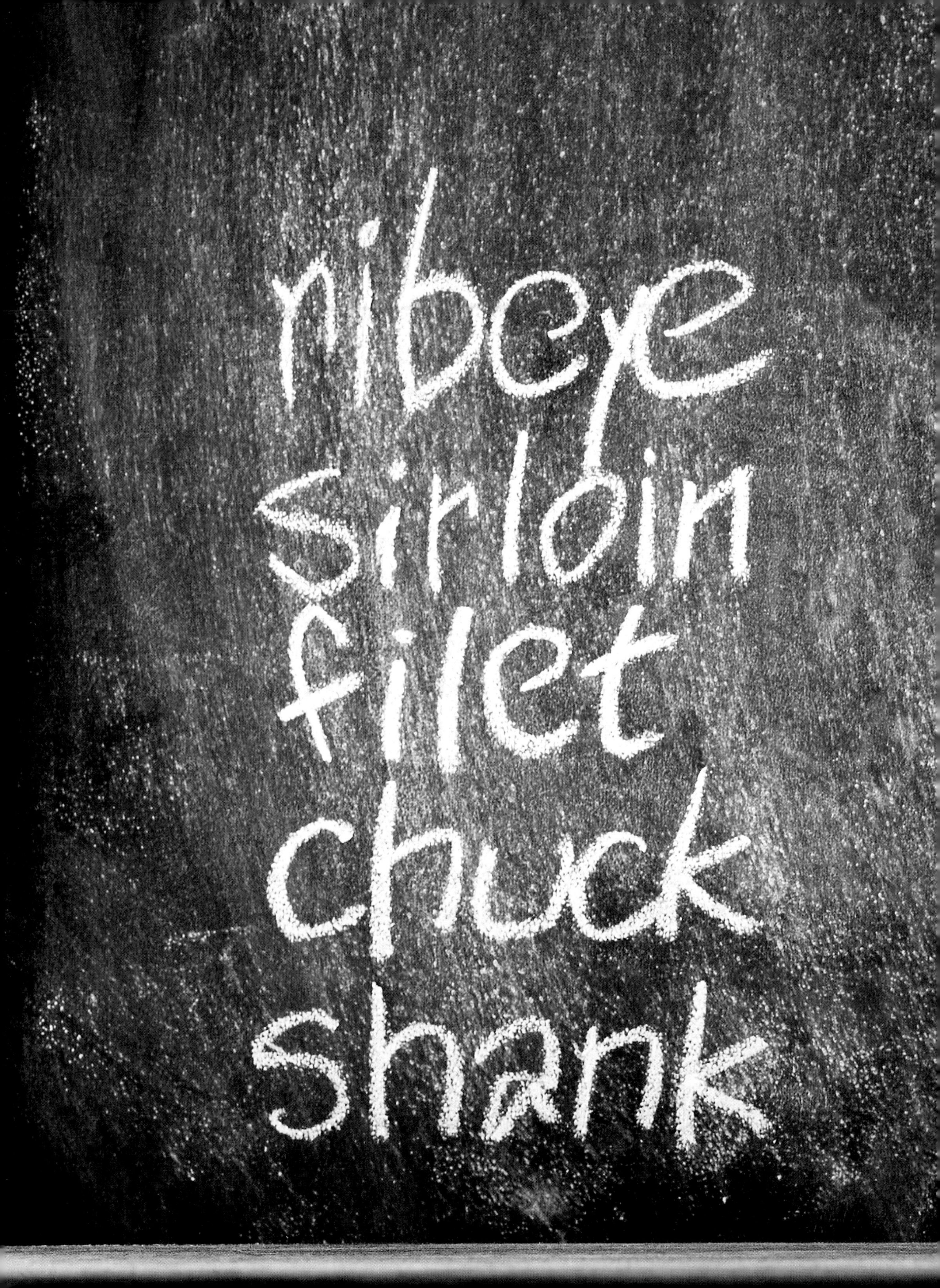

ribeye
sirloin
filet
chuck
shank

BEEF

BACKYARD BURGERS WITH THE WORKS

The infinite array of burger flavors out there today are all based on simple grilled or griddled ground beef meaty deliciousness. Lightly handled. Juicy yet seared. An excellent burger at heart. Then you get to indulge your burger topping fantasies, or you can just chill out and stick to this old-school classic. SERVES 4

For the burgers

1 to 1½ pounds (450 to 675 g) of ground fatty chuck

2 teaspoons (10 mL) of salt

Lots of freshly ground pepper

For the works

4 sturdy buns, kaiser rolls or the like, not soft and flimsy run-of-the-mill buns

2 tablespoons (30 mL) or so of butter, softened

4 or 8 thick slices of Cheddar or your favorite cheese

A few large leaves of fresh crisp lettuce

1 ripe red tomato, sliced

1 red onion, thinly sliced

2 large classic dill pickles, sliced

A few squirts of ketchup

A few spoonfuls of Dijon mustard

A few spoonfuls of green relish

Build a hardwood fire and let it die down to a thick bed of glowing coals, or prepare and preheat your barbecue, grill, or griddle to its highest setting.

Split the rolls in half and thoroughly butter the inside of each one. Next, form the burgers. Divide the beef into quarters. Shape each portion into an even burger about an inch (2.5 cm) thick. Season both sides with salt and pepper. Press a noticeable depression into the center of each burger. This will help the burger shrink evenly as the meat cooks through; the hollow will eventually disappear.

Grill or griddle the burgers until the bottom is seared and crispy, about 5 minutes. Resist the urge to press on the burgers with your spatula; this just encourages them to release valuable juices and flavor. Flip and continue cooking until the burger is cooked through to your liking. If you're not sure of their doneness, do what every line cook does their first day on the job: make a small cut and have a look. In the last minute or so, drape a cheese slice or two over each burger.

Meanwhile, grill, griddle, or toast the buttered burger buns until they're golden brown and toasty. Arrange them on your work surface, pairing bottoms with tops. Layer the tops first with the lettuce, then the tomato, red onion, and pickle slices. Place the grilled burgers directly on the toasted bottoms so they absorb any juices. Smear the burgers with ketchup, mustard, and green relish. Slide the lettuce stack from the top of the bun to the top of the burger. Top with the bun and get to servin' and sharin'!

> **TWIST**
>
> Once you've mastered this basic method you can start to experiment and build your own custom burgers. Try out different breads, cheeses, condiments, and garnishes. There's no right and wrong as long as you're having fun and plates are getting licked clean!

IRON STEAK FOR THE TABLE

This is an impressive steak, 32 ounces of the most delicious, juicy, and beautifully browned steak. Serve this to a bunch of really hungry people. It's for sharing, and it's a lot easier to cook this much beef in one big piece in one big pan. A skillet sear first, then an oven roast finish— works every time! SERVES 4

Allow the steak to rest at room temperature for at least 1 hour before cooking. Preheat your oven to 400°F (200°C) and turn on your convection fan if you have one.

Heat a 10- or 12-inch (25 or 30 cm) cast-iron skillet over medium-high heat until it's searing hot and sizzling, 5 minutes or so. Meanwhile, place your steak on a large platter and rub the oil evenly all over it. Season the steak liberally and evenly with the salt and pepper.

Carefully place the steak in the sizzling-hot pan and sear it, without moving it, until browned and crusty on both sides, 5 minutes or so per side. Prop the steak up on one of the unseared sides and immediately transfer it to the oven.

After 10 minutes, jab a meat thermometer into the thickest part of the steak. If it's hitting your mark on the scale (see the Twist), pull it from the oven. If not, roast it for another few minutes. Continue until you get to your desired doneness.

Transfer the steak to a cutting board and tent it loosely with foil. Let it rest for at least 10 minutes to allow the vital juices to cool and calm down so they don't flow out when you cut into the meat. (Leave the thermometer in the meat and you'll notice that it continues cooking and rises a bit farther on the scale.) Slice, serve, and share!

A 32- to 48-ounce (900 g to 1.35 kg) New York strip loin steak (3 to 4 inches/8 to 10 cm thick)

A few tablespoons (30 to 45 mL) of vegetable oil

1 teaspoon (5 mL) of coarse salt

Lots of freshly ground pepper

TWIST

The best way to protect your investment and guarantee beef doneness is with an accurate thermometer. Roast the meat to the temperature shown below, then pull it from the oven. As it rests it will rise a few more degrees, finish cooking, and relax into the zone shown.

RARE	PULL AT 110°F (43°C)
MEDIUM-RARE	PULL AT 120°F (50°C)
MEDIUM	PULL AT 130°F (55°C)
MEDIUM-WELL	PULL AT 140°F (60°C)

BRAZILIAN GRILLED STEAK WITH SALSA CRIOLLA

The *churrasco* service style of a Brazilian steakhouse is one of the world's great food experiences. Spice-rubbed, slow-roasted tender beef is thinly sliced at the table and served with bright, spicy condiments like the ubiquitous salsa criolla. The big, bold flavors of South America are easily found in your kitchen too. SERVES 4, WITH LOTS OF LEFTOVER SALSA CRIOLLA

For the salsa criolla

2 garlic cloves

1 jalapeño pepper, quartered and seeded

½ cup (125 mL) of your favorite red wine vinegar

¼ cup (60 mL) of your best extra-virgin olive oil

1 teaspoon (5 mL) of dried oregano

1 teaspoon (5 mL) of salt

1 green bell pepper, chopped

1 red onion, thinly sliced

2 pints (1 L) of cherry tomatoes, halved

Leaves and tender stems from 1 bunch of fresh cilantro, flat-leaf parsley, or both, chopped

For the steaks

1 tablespoon (15 mL) of ground cumin

1 tablespoon (15 mL) of garlic powder

1 tablespoon (15 mL) of onion powder

1 tablespoon (15 mL) of dry mustard

1 tablespoon (15 mL) of ground oregano

1 tablespoon (15 mL) of salt

4 thick rib-eye, New York strip loin, flank, hanger, or your favorite beef steaks

Build a hardwood fire and let it die down to a thick bed of glowing coals, or preheat your barbecue, grill, or griddle to its highest setting.

Craft the salsa. It's great freshly made but best when it rest overnight. Fill your food processor with the garlic, jalapeño pepper, vinegar, oil, oregano, and salt. Pulse the intense ingredients for a few moments until smooth. Add the bell pepper, then process until the ingredients are coarsely chopped and the consistency of salsa.

In a medium bowl, toss together the onion and cherry tomatoes. Add the fresh herb leaves and tender aromatic stems, then pour the salsa over the works. Toss everything together, forming a rustic condiment that will only get better as it rests for a few hours or even a few days.

Prepare the steaks. Measure the seasonings into a small jar with a tight-fitting lid. Shake the works to blend. Sprinkle each side of each steak with 2 teaspoons (10 mL) of the spice blend, gently massaging the spice into the meat. Grill the steaks, turning once or twice, until they're seared and medium-rare, about 5 minutes per side. Serve and share with lots of salsa criolla and a sharp steak knife for everyone. Encourage lots of slicing, dipping, and slurping with a big red Argentinean wine.

-------- **TWIST** --------
The relentless quest to grill local meat is nearly universal, always locally distinctive, and almost always delicious. The street-food peddlers and steakhouses of the world are fonts of food traditions and flavor ideas. They show how cooks the world over can experiment and create.

MEATBALL STEAKS WITH RED WINE MUSHROOM STEW

This is not your grandmother's meatball recipe, but it does showcase the classic beefy flavors of rich, aromatic meatballs. In this case the meatball mix is shaped into a thick steak, grilled to perfection, then smothered with a delicious mushroom stew. I really don't think your grandma would mind, though. SERVES 4

Begin with the mushroom stew. Heat a large skillet over medium-high heat. Toss in the butter and swirl it for a few moments as it melts. Add the mushrooms, onion, and garlic; sauté until the aromatic vegetables soften, release and lose lots of moisture, and thicken, 10 to 15 minutes. Season the works with thyme, salt, and pepper. Pour in the red wine. Continue cooking, stirring occasionally, until the wine and liquid reduce by half or more, about 10 minutes. When the stew has thickened, stir in the cream and oregano. Continue cooking until heated through, just a few minutes more. Remove from heat and keep warm.

For the meatball steaks, in a large bowl combine the ground beef, eggs, onion, garlic, ketchup, oregano, soy sauce, and Worcestershire. Mix together gently with your hands until everything is thoroughly combined. Divide the mixture into quarters. Shape each portion into an oval "steak" about an inch (2.5 cm) thick. Transfer to a plate.

Heat your favorite large skillet over medium-high heat until it's sizzling hot, 5 minutes or so. Add a generous splash of vegetable oil, covering the bottom of the pan. Carefully place the steaks in the pan. Sear until the bottom is browned and crusty, about 5 minutes. Resist the urge to press on the steaks with your spatula. This just releases delicious juices and thus flavor. Flip the steaks and continue to cook until they are just cooked through, another 5 minutes or so. Serve and share with lots of ladles of mushroom stew!

For the mushroom stew

2 tablespoons (30 mL) of butter

1 pound (450 g) of white or other mushrooms, sliced

1 large onion, diced

4 garlic cloves, thinly sliced

1 teaspoon (5 mL) of dried thyme

½ teaspoon (2 mL) of salt

Lots of freshly ground pepper

1 cup (250 mL) or so of your favorite red wine

1 cup (250 mL) of whipping cream

Leaves from 1 bunch of fresh oregano, chopped

For the meatball steaks

1½ pounds (675 g) of ground beef

2 eggs, whisked

1 large onion, shredded on a box grater

4 or 5 garlic cloves, minced

¼ cup (60 mL) of ketchup

2 tablespoons (30 mL) of dried oregano

1 tablespoon (15 mL) of soy sauce

1 teaspoon (5 mL) of Worcestershire sauce

2 tablespoons (30 mL) of vegetable oil

TWIST

Feel free to use a mixture of mushrooms in this dish. There are many these days and here's a great place to show them off. You can experiment with the ground meat as well. Try substituting ground pork or bulk sausage for some of the beef. A 100% ground turkey works nicely here too.

STEAK BURRITOS WITH BARBECUE BEANS

For most of the world, steak is a condiment—a little goes a long way. In these burritos, the beefy grilled flavors meet their meaty match in the barbecue beans. Together the beef and beans anchor these hefty, hearty burritos. SERVES 6

For the beans

1 tablespoon (15 mL) of
    extra-virgin olive oil

1 large onion, diced

1 large red bell pepper, finely diced

4 garlic cloves, sliced

A 19-ounce (540 mL) can of
    mixed beans, drained and rinsed

1 tablespoon (15 mL) of
    chili powder

½ cup (125 mL) or so of
    your favorite barbecue sauce

For the steaks

2 of your favorite thick steaks,
    beef or pork

½ teaspoon (2 mL) of salt

Lots of freshly ground pepper

For the burritos

6 large flour tortillas

6 ounces (170 g) or so of
    taco blend cheese

4 green onions, sliced

Leaves from 1 bunch of
    fresh cilantro

------- **TWIST** -------
Substitute a shredded store-bought rotisserie chicken for the steak in these burritos. Once you've mastered the simple art of rolling a burrito tightly, the filling inside is limited only by your imagination.

Start with the beans. Heat your favorite large skillet over medium heat. Splash in the olive oil, and when it's hot, toss in the onion, bell pepper, and garlic; sauté until they soften and lightly brown, 5 minutes or so. Stir in the beans, chili powder, and barbecue sauce. Simmer until everything is warmed through and delicious, another few minutes.

For the steaks, build a hardwood fire and let it burn down to a thick bed of glowing hot coals, or prepare and preheat your grill or barbecue to its highest setting.

When you're ready to grill, pat the steaks dry with paper towels and season both sides liberally with salt and pepper. Position the steaks on the grill. After a few minutes, turn the steaks over and grill for a few more minutes until the steak reaches the doneness you prefer. Transfer the steaks to a cutting board and let them rest for a few minutes to help them relax and retain vital moisture and flavor. Thinly slice the steaks.

To assemble the burritos, arrange the tortillas on your work surface. Arrange some of the steak slices evenly in a line across the middle of each tortilla, without going all the way to the edges. Top the steak slices evenly with the barbecue beans, staying away from the edges of the tortilla. Finally top the works with the cheese, green onions, and lots of cilantro. Working with 1 burrito at a time, fold up the bottom until it almost covers the filling, then fold in the sides. Roll the burrito up tightly. Let it rest seam side down. Repeat with the remaining burritos.

For extra flair and flash, place the burritos seam side down on the still-hot grill and toast them lightly, about 3 minutes. Flip and repeat on the opposite side. Serve and share!

BEEF POT PIE WITH CHEDDAR BISCUIT CRUST

Slow, patient braising transforms an inexpensive cut of stewing beef into a rich, tender stew. A cheesy biscuit crust then transforms the works into a special occasion. From tough beef to delectable meal—that's transformation! SERVES 4 TO 6

Begin the stew. Heat your largest thick-bottomed ovenproof pot over medium-high heat. While the pot is heating, pat the beef dry with paper towels. Splash enough oil into your pot to cover the bottom with a thin film. Carefully add just enough beef for a single sizzling layer—don't crowd the pan and slow down the flavorful heat. Keep the pan's heat high enough to sizzle and sear the meat until it's brown on all sides, 10 minutes or so per batch. Use a slotted spoon to transfer the beef to a plate as it's done. Pour off any excess fat but retain all the crispy browned flavor bits.

Return the beef and any juices to the pan, then pour in the tomatoes and the bottle of red wine, covering the works. Season with the bay leaves, rosemary, salt, and pepper. Bring to a slow, steady simmer, then cover and simmer for 30 minutes or so.

Stir in the carrots, parsnips, potatoes, onions, and turnip. Continue simmering, covered, until the meat is tender and tasty, another 30 minutes or so. At the last minute stir in lots of color and flavor with the frozen peas. Transfer the stew to a festive baking dish if you wish.

Meanwhile, begin the biscuits. Preheat the oven to 400°F (200°C) and turn on your convection fan if you have one. In a large bowl, whisk together the flour, baking powder, and salt. Stir the Cheddar cheese into the dry ingredients. Grate the frozen butter through the large holes of a box grater directly into the dry ingredients. Gently toss the works together with your fingers until the butter and cheese shards are spread evenly throughout the flour.

Continued

For the beef stew
2 pounds (900 g) of stewing beef, cut in 1-inch (2.5 cm) cubes

A splash of vegetable oil

A 28-ounce (796 mL) can of whole tomatoes

1 bottle (750 mL) or so of your favorite hearty red wine

A few bay leaves

A few sprigs of fresh rosemary

½ teaspoon (2 mL) of salt

Lots of freshly ground pepper

2 carrots, chopped

2 parsnips or a sweet potato, chopped

2 potatoes, peeled and cubed

2 onions, chopped

1 turnip, peeled and chopped

A few handfuls of frozen peas

For the Cheddar cheese biscuits
4 cups (1 L) of all-purpose flour

2 tablespoons (30 mL) of baking powder

2 teaspoons (10 mL) of salt

1 cup (250 mL) of shredded Cheddar cheese

½ cup (125 mL) of rock-hard frozen butter

1½ cups (375 mL) of milk

Pour in the milk and stir with the handle of a wooden spoon until a dough mass forms. (The handle of the spoon is gentler on the dough.) Fold the dough over in the bowl a few times with your hands until all the ingredients are gathered up and come together. If necessary add a spoonful or two more milk to help incorporate any stray flour. A bit of gentle kneading doesn't toughen the biscuits but strengthens the dough and helps a crisp crust form as the biscuits bake.

Gently pull small pieces of the biscuit from the dough ball and place them on top of the finished beef stew, nestling them all in together and doubling up as needed. Cover and bake for 30 minutes or so until the biscuits are tender and the stew is fragrant and bubbly. Serve and share!

TWIST

The most important step in braising beef is browning it thoroughly at the start, while the pan's heat is high and before the liquids lower the temperature. Once you master browning you get to experiment with the other side of braising: crafting a flavorful, aromatic liquid to simmer the meat in. Stirring in your personality as you go. Trying new flavor ideas.

BEEFY RED WINE BRAISED BEEF SHANKS

Nothing is packed with more rich beef flavor than a beef shank, but it does take a bit of patient encouragement to release that flavor. A bottle of beefy red wine and a slow cooker will get the job done and you'll be rewarded with a delicious dinner. SERVES 4

Heat your favorite heavy skillet over medium-high heat. Splash in the oil, and when it's hot, sear the beef shanks until they're browned all over, about 5 minutes per side. This is your only chance to add high-heat flavor before the low-heat simmer ahead. Remove from the heat.

Into your slow cooker, pile the onions, garlic, carrots, prunes, rosemary, peppercorns, salt, and bay leaves; pour in the wine. Stir the works, then nestle in the beef shanks. Cover and cook on High for 6 hours or on Low for 8 hours. The moist heat will slowly tenderize the meat while releasing its rich flavor. Fish out the bone pieces, stir the works together, then ladle over your favorite potato, rice, or noodles. Serve and share!

A splash of vegetable oil

A pair of 6- to 8-ounce (170 to 225 g) cross-cut bone-in beef shanks

2 onions, chopped

4 garlic cloves, peeled

2 carrots, chopped

1 cup (250 mL) of pitted prunes

2 or 3 large sprigs of fresh rosemary

1 teaspoon (5 mL) of black peppercorns

1 teaspoon (5 mL) of salt

1 or 2 bay leaves

1 bottle (750 mL) of your favorite big-flavored Zinfandel, Syrah, Cabernet, or other hearty red wine

```
------------------ TWIST ------------------
 There are many tough, inexpensive cuts of meat at your
 butcher that need braising to release their rich flavor, such
 as short ribs or any stewing meat like top round, bottom
 round, or eye of round. Sear them for initial brown flavor,
 then submerge in simmering aromatic liquid and you're
 braising. The classic technique is easy to master, and it's
 easy to stir in your own freestyle ideas too. Prunes dis-
 solve easily into the sauce, adding full flavor and body, but
 dried tomatoes, olives, and mushrooms work well too. Try
 different herbs; stronger flavors, such as sage, thyme, and
 oregano, all add distinctive character. Choose a favorite
 wine, then create your own stew!
```

BIG NOODLES WITH MEATY TOMATO SAUCE

Braising inexpensive beef shanks in tomato sauce is an excellent way to add big, beefy flavor to a simple pasta dish. But what if you love slow, patient flavors and don't have time to wait? Put away your old-school pot and speed things up with a spiffy pressure cooker. You'll be amazed at how fast and easy today's pressure cookers are, and safe too. They're an excellent addition to your kitchen. SERVES 4 TO 6

2 tablespoons (30 mL) of
   vegetable oil

A pair of 6- to 8-ounce (170 to 225 g)
   bone-in beef shanks

2 onions, chopped

4 garlic cloves, sliced

2 carrots, chopped

1 cup (250 mL) of your
   favorite red wine

A 28-ounce (796 mL) can of
   whole or diced tomatoes

2 bay leaves

2 tablespoons (30 mL) of
   dried oregano

1 teaspoon (5 mL) of salt

1 pound (450 g) of rigatoni or
   your favorite pasta

½ cup (125 mL) of pitted
   kalamata olives

10 ounces (280 g) of fresh
   baby spinach

Place your pressure cooker over medium-high heat and splash in the vegetable oil. When the oil is hot, sear the beef shanks until they're browned all over, about 5 minutes per side. This is your only chance to add high-heat flavor before the low-heat simmer ahead. Remove the shanks and rest on a plate.

Turn off the heat and toss in the onions, garlic, and carrots. Pour in the red wine and the tomatoes, breaking up any whole ones with your fingers. Season the sauce with the bay leaves, oregano, and salt. Return the browned shanks to the pot. Bring the works to a full boil, then reduce the heat to low, just enough to maintain a simmer. Fit the lid onto the pot, forming a tight seal. Cook at full pressure, allowing the intense internal pressure to dramatically speed up tenderizing while preserving flavor and nutrients, for about 20 minutes. Meanwhile, bring a large pot of salted water to a boil and start cooking your pasta.

Turn off the heat and let the pressure cooker rest, allowing the steam to die down completely before carefully removing the lid when the noodles are finished. Fish out the shank bones, breaking up the meat as you go, then stir in the olives and spinach. Ladle the sauce over the just-drained pasta. Serve and share!

------------------------ **TWIST** ------------------------
Pressure cookers are back! Use one once and you'll realize that it's a safe and easy way to get a tasty, healthy dinner on the table in a hurry. Because the pressure seals the pot so tight, many of the aromas and nutrients that are lost in other cooking methods stay sealed in the food. Bottom line? Pressure cookers are faster, tastier, and healthier.

BEEF POT ROAST WITH AROMATIC VEGETABLE GRAVY

Pot-roasting is an easy way to reliably cook a large beef roast and create a full meal in a pot. This dish harnesses the power of slow cooking to melt beef and cook potatoes. Best of all, you can quickly create smooth gravy from the cooking juices and aromatic vegetables by puréeing the works in a blender. SERVES 4 TO 6

Preheat your oven to 350°F (180°C) and turn on your convection fan if you have one.

Heat a large Dutch oven or heavy stew pot over medium heat. Toss in 2 tablespoons (30 mL) of the butter, then the onion, carrot, and celery. Gently cook, stirring occasionally, until their colors brighten and their flavors deepen, about 10 minutes. Pour in the tomatoes, red wine, bay leaves, and rosemary. Nestle in the roast and bring the works to a simmer. Turn off the heat, nestle the potatoes around the roast, and cover with a tight-fitting lid. Transfer to the oven. Reduce the oven temperature to 300°F (150°C) and patiently simmer the pot roast for 4 hours.

After enduring hours of delicious aromas, transfer the potatoes to a serving bowl and the roast to a platter or cutting board. Cover the meat with tented foil and let it rest. Transfer the remaining vegetables and juice to a blender and carefully purée. Alternatively, speed cleanup and purée with an immersion blender directly in the pot. Either way, reheat the smooth, thick gravy in the pot; whisk in the remaining 1 tablespoon (15 mL) butter for added richness. Slice the roast, serve alongside the potatoes, and share the works with ladles of tasty gravy!

3 tablespoons (45 mL) of butter

1 large onion, diced

1 large carrot, diced

2 celery ribs, diced

A 19-ounce (540 mL) can of diced tomatoes

1 cup (250 mL) or so of your favorite red wine

2 bay leaves

2 or 3 large sprigs of fresh rosemary

A large beef pot roast, 4 pounds (1.8 kg) or so

8 medium potatoes or 24 baby potatoes

- - - - - - - - - - - **TWIST** - - - - - - - - - - -

This is neither a stew nor a braise. In this dish the meat is not browned and it rests well above the surrounding liquid. Even though the pot is covered, the exposed meat still browns; it just takes a long time. Along the way the meat not only gains a lot of flavor but also releases much of its moisture into the pot, hence the need to create a gravy to moisten up your plate.

ANCHO CHILI MAC 'N' CHEESE

Cooking for a crowd? This two-part dish is a great choice. It features a deeply flavored authentic chili that you can optionally stretch into an even bigger meal by stirring in mac and cheese. Either way, you'll be rewarded with lots of soul-satisfying big flavor. SERVES 6 TO 8

For the ancho chili

A 4-pound (1.8 kg) chuck roast, trimmed and cut in 1-inch (2.5 cm) cubes

Several splashes of vegetable oil

2 onions, chopped

Cloves from 1 head of garlic, chopped

1 tablespoon (15 mL) of dried oregano

1 tablespoon (15 mL) of ground cumin

1 teaspoon (5 mL) of cinnamon

1 teaspoon (5 mL) of salt

2 ancho chilies, broken or chopped into pieces

A couple of 28-ounce (796 mL) cans of whole tomatoes

A 19-ounce (540 mL) can of red kidney beans, drained and rinsed

A 19-ounce (540 mL) can of black beans, drained and rinsed

For the mac and cheese

2 cups (500 mL) of elbow macaroni

3 cups (750 mL) of water

2 cups (500 mL) of taco blend cheese

For the chili, heat a large, heavy pot over medium-high heat. While the pot is heating, pat the beef dry with paper towels. Splash enough oil into your pot to cover the bottom with a thin film. Carefully add just enough beef for a single sizzling layer—don't crowd the pan and slow down the flavorful heat. Keep the pan's heat high enough to sizzle and sear the meat until it's brown on all sides, 10 minutes or so per batch. Use a slotted spoon to transfer the beef to a plate as it's done. Add the onions and garlic to the pan and cook, stirring, just long enough to heat them through and brighten their flavors, 2 or 3 minutes. Add the oregano, cumin, cinnamon, salt, and ancho chilies; stir for a few minutes. Return the browned beef and any juices to the pan along with the tomatoes and beans. Bring to a full boil, then reduce the heat to a slow simmer. Cover and simmer, stirring occasionally, until the beef is flavorful and tender, about 1 hour.

When the chili is tender you may serve and share it right away or you can really amp up the dish with Mac 'n' Cheese. Preheat your oven to 375°F (190°C) and turn on your convection fan if you have one. Add the macaroni and water to the chili over medium-low heat. Stir for a few minutes as the water heats through and the macaroni begins cooking. Stir half of the cheese blend into the chili, then pour the works into a 13- × 9-inch (3 L) baking pan. Top with the remaining cheese. Bake your masterpiece until it's bubbly and lightly browned, 15 minutes or so. Serve, share, and graciously accept all the compliments!

FEARLESS PRIME RIB

A prime rib roast can be intimidating. It's big and expensive and seemingly hard to cook, but if you can dedicate an oven to the project for a few hours you can easily cook this king of meats with spectacular results. The secret is to begin with high heat and finish with low heat.

SERVES 4 TO 8

Rest your roast at room temperature for at least 3 hours. It's much easier to bring it up to room temperature on the counter than in the oven, and once it's cooking it won't have as long to go. Make sure you have a sharp slicing knife ready.

Position a rack toward the bottom of the oven so the meat will roast in the middle. Preheat the oven to 500°F (260°C) and turn on your convection fan if you have one.

Sprinkle the entire surface of the roast with salt, pepper, and flour. Massage in the works. Don't worry if it doesn't all adhere—the flour will still help form a crispy crust. Position the roast in your favorite roasting pan with the fat side up and bone side down. Transfer to the hot, hot oven. Close the oven door and leave it closed. Don't peek! Post a guard if you need to, because this method relies on keeping all the heat in the oven.

Cook a 4-bone roast for 1 hour, a 3-bone for 45 minutes, and a 2-bone for 30 minutes. Without opening the oven, turn off the heat and wait 2 full hours more. During this time the initial high browning heat will dissipate and the roast will slowly finish cooking at lower, juicier temperatures.

After 2 patient hours, open the oven and you'll be rewarded with a perfectly cooked prime rib roast in the medium-rare to medium range. It will be beautifully browned on the outside yet moist, juicy, and red-pink on the inside. Transfer the roast to a platter or a cutting board with the bones upright and facing away from you. First make a series of small guide incisions in the fat side, evenly dividing the meat into serving portions, before you commit to full slicing. Then slice down confidently all the way through the meat to the bone. Look closer and decide which side of the bone to cut against to free each slice. Not every piece will have a bone attached, but every piece will benefit from being roasted on the bone. They just plain taste better! Serve and share!

A 2-bone, 3-bone, or 4-bone standing prime rib roast

A few teaspoons (10 mL or so) of salt

Lots of freshly ground pepper

½ cup (125 mL) or so of whole wheat flour

TWIST

Prime rib is traditionally served with sharp horseradish, which is easy to freestyle. Craft your own side sauce by simply stirring together two parts mayonnaise or sour cream with one part prepared horseradish and a few of your favorite freestyle flourishes: chop in some fresh herbs like tarragon or thyme, or stir in Worcestershire sauce, soy sauce, ketchup, or grainy mustard. Pickles work well too, whether in standard green relish or simply chopped. And capers are good. The sky's the limit!

STREET BEEF SALAD WITH ASIAN FLAVORS

This is quite possibly the most delicious beef dish I've ever had the pleasure of gathering, preparing, and sharing. It's inspired by a variety of street foods that I enjoyed in Thailand, yet it's not meant to be authentically Thai. It's just authentically delicious to ladle an exotically spiced beef broth over a bright, crisp salad. It's also authentic to speed things up with a pressure cooker. SERVES 4 TO 6

For the beef

2 cups (500 mL) of orange juice

1 cup (250 mL) of orange marmalade

½ cup (125 mL) of fish sauce

¼ cup (60 mL) of sambal oelek or your favorite chili-garlic sauce

6 or 8 lime leaves

3-inch (8 cm) piece of fresh ginger (unpeeled), thinly sliced

1 tablespoon (15 mL) of cinnamon

A roughly 4-pound (1.8 kg) beef pot roast, cut in 1- or 2-inch (2.5 or 5 cm) cubes

For the salad

An 8-ounce (227 g) package or a few handfuls of fresh bean sprouts

A few handfuls of fresh baby spinach

1 large carrot, peeled into ribbons with a vegetable peeler

2 mangoes, peeled and sliced into thin strips

24 snow peas, thinly sliced

1 red onion, thinly sliced

1 bunch of fresh cilantro, ripped and torn (not chopped)

Begin with the beef. In your pressure cooker, combine the orange juice, marmalade, fish sauce, sambal, lime leaves, ginger, and cinnamon. Bring everything to a full boil over medium-high heat, then stir in the beef. Bring the works back to a full boil, then reduce the heat enough to maintain a bare simmer. Fit the lid onto the pot, forming a tight seal. Cook at full pressure, allowing the intense internal pressure to dramatically speed up tenderizing and flavor, for 20 minutes. Turn off the heat and let rest for a few minutes, allowing the steam to die down completely before carefully removing the lid.

To make the salad, in a large bowl toss together the bean sprouts, spinach, carrot, mango, snow peas, and onion. Divide the proceeds evenly among several festive serving bowls or, for even more fun, a few Chinese takeout containers.

Top the salad with steaming ladlefuls of the aromatic stew. Garnish with handfuls of cilantro, poke in a pair of chopsticks if you dare, and serve and share!

TWIST

Cooks all over the world routinely transform tough, inexpensive beef into tender, locally flavored cuisine. You can do so quickly with a super-efficient pressure cooker. If you don't have one, just pile the same ingredients into a standard-issue pot and simmer patiently for an hour or so until the meat inevitably tenderizes.

PORK & LAMB

HARVEST PORK CHOPS

Pork chops are best cooked by first searing them on one side, then flipping them over, covering tightly, and finishing on a gentle heat. At heart this beautiful dish is anchored by that basic method, which allows for a few extravagant fall-flavor flourishes to get thrown in too.

SERVES 2 TO 4

For the stuffed pork chops

2 extra-thick pork loin chops

1 of your favorite Italian sausages, casing removed

1 tablespoon (15 mL) of minced fresh rosemary

1 heaping tablespoon (18 mL) of whole-berry cranberry sauce

1 tablespoon (15 mL) of grainy mustard

A splash of vegetable oil

For the cranberry kale stew

1 onion, chopped

4 garlic cloves, chopped

½ cup (125 mL) of cranberry cocktail

½ cup (125 mL) of whole-berry cranberry sauce

1 tablespoon (15 mL) of grainy mustard

½ teaspoon (2 mL) of salt

1 bunch of kale (roughly 1 pound/450 g), center stems discarded, thinly sliced

Start by stuffing the pork chops. Carefully slice each chop in half horizontally, cutting it open like a book and leaving a thick hinge on one side. In a medium bowl, combine the sausage meat, rosemary, cranberry sauce, and grainy mustard; mix well. Neatly stuff each chop with an even layer of the sausage mixture, then fold the meat back together.

Heat a large, heavy skillet over medium-high heat. Splash in the oil, enough to coat the bottom with a thin film. When it's hot, sear the chops until they're golden brown and crispy on each side, 3 to 4 minutes per side. Transfer the chops to a plate and loosely cover with foil.

To make the kale stew, add the onion and garlic to the hot pan and sauté for a minute or two. Stir in the cranberry juice, cranberry sauce, mustard, and salt; bring to a simmer. Add half the kale. Stir while it wilts, in just a minute or so. Nestle the chops back in and top with the remaining kale. Pour in any juices from the plate, then cover tightly and continue cooking until the chops reach an internal temperature of 145°F (65°C), about 10 minutes. Mound the kale stew on your dinner plates and top with a stuffed pork chop, whole or thickly sliced. Serve and share!

TWIST

This hearty dish works well with any savory green—Asian greens, spinach, Swiss chard, mustard greens, or beet greens. The cranberry flavors can easily become orange with juice and marmalade making an appearance. A strong tomato theme works well here too. Get creative!

PAN-RUSHED PORK CHOPS

Sear, sauce, and simmer—the three basic steps of pan-rushing. An initial high-heat sear for true brown flavor, a sauce of distinctive aromatic flavor built in the same pan, then a slow simmer that simultaneously finishes both the meat and the sauce. A masterful method with infinite openings for flavor themes. SERVES 2

Match your favorite large skillet with a tight-fitting lid and medium-high heat. Splash in enough vegetable oil to evenly cover the bottom of the pan. Sear the chops until they're golden brown and crusty on each side, 2 or 3 minutes per side. The goal here is not to fully cook the meat but just to add lots of brown flavor while the pan's temperature is still high. Transfer the chops to a plate and cover loosely with foil.

Lower the pan's heat to medium. Toss in the onion and garlic; sauté for a minute or two, softening textures and awakening flavors. Follow with the mushrooms, salt, and pepper. Continue cooking for another few minutes. Swirl in the wine and vigorously simmer until the liquid is reduced by at least half, 3 minutes or so. Swirl in the cream, then lower the heat to maintain a slow, steady simmer.

Return the chops and any juices to the pan, nestling them into the creamy mushrooms. Cover tightly and continue cooking the meat and stewing the mushrooms. Cook until the chops reach an internal temperature of at least 145°F (65°C), just 5 minutes or so. Finish the dish by stirring in the tarragon at the last second to preserve its sharp, fresh flavor. Divvy up the chops and smother them with ladles of the mushroom stew. Serve and share!

A splash of vegetable oil

2 thick pork chops, with or without bone

1 onion, sliced

4 cloves of garlic, minced

8 ounces (225 g) of whole button mushrooms, halved or quartered if large

½ teaspoon (2 mL) of salt

½ teaspoon (2 mL) of pepper

1 cup (250 mL) of your favorite red wine

½ cup (125 mL) of whipping cream or sour cream

Leaves from 1 bunch of fresh tarragon, chopped

TWIST

This dish is perfect for freestyling your own flavors. Your choice of wine, fruit or vegetable, and fresh herb all offer signature opportunities. Change the mushrooms to any fruit, complement with your favorite fully flavored wine, and experiment with your aromatic herb choices and you'll be well on your way to creating a new dish all your own.

SLOW CHILI-RUBBED RIBS

Pork ribs are best when cooked with patience. They'll easily relax and tenderize with long, slow cooking and memorable flavoring. Be aggressive with your flavors, seal the works tightly to keep them from drying out, be patient as they slowly soften and tenderize, and in time you'll be rewarded with gold-standard flavor. SERVES 2 TO 4

2 racks of baby back pork ribs

½ cup (125 mL) of brown sugar

½ cup (125 mL) of ground ancho chilies or your favorite chili powder

1 tablespoon (15 mL) of ground cumin

1 tablespoon (15 mL) of dried oregano

1 teaspoon (5 mL) of cinnamon

Preheat your oven to 400°F (200°C) and turn on your convection fan if you have one.

Prepare the ribs. Most pork rib racks have a tough, indigestible membrane—called the fell—on their bone side. Use a spoon to loosen this membrane, then grasp it tightly and peel it off. This will help the ribs tenderize and cook evenly. (You can also ask your friendly neighborhood butcher to do this for you.) Cut each rack into 2 equal pieces.

Whisk together the sugar, ground ancho, cumin, oregano, and cinnamon. Evenly rub the mix over and into both sides of all the ribs. Fit the ribs into a large baking pan, overlapping and fitting as needed to evenly fill the pan. If your baking pan doesn't have a tight-fitting lid, place one long sheet of foil over another the same length. Fold over one long side by ½ inch (1 cm) and crimp tightly; fold and crimp another ½ inch. Open up the two sheets into one larger one and tightly crease the center seam. Cover the pan, crimping the edges tightly. This craftsmanship really helps preserve vital moisture in the meat.

Place the pan in the oven and lower the temperature to 300°F (150°C). Bake slowly until the meat is beautifully browned, highly aromatic, and meltingly tender, about 3 hours. At the table remove the foil with a flourish and divvy up the spoils within.

```
----------------------  TWIST  -------------------------
  Ribs benefit from the two basic parts of this cooking method.
  Slow, sealed baking guarantees tenderness and juiciness.
  Aggressive flavoring makes it all worthwhile. Become a slow
  master so you can create your own spice blends for slowly
  baking, tenderizing, and ultimately flavoring the ribs.
-----------------------------------------------------------
```

SLOW-BAKED HONEY MUSTARD RIBS

Pork ribs automatically tenderize when they're sealed tight and baked slowly. They happily absorb whatever flavors happen to be along for the ride too. Honey and mustard are perfect for the long haul and make for finger-licking good ribs. SERVES 4

Preheat your oven to 400°F (200°C) and turn on your convection fan if you have one.

Prepare the ribs. Most pork rib racks have a tough, indigestible membrane—called the fell—on their bone side. Use a spoon to loosen this membrane, then grasp it tightly and peel it off. This will help the ribs tenderize and cook evenly. (You can also ask your friendly neighborhood butcher to do this for you.) Cut each rack into 2 equal pieces.

Whisk together the honey, mustard, thyme, and salt. Pour the sauce over both sides of the ribs, evenly coating them. Fit the ribs into a large baking pan, overlapping and fitting as needed to evenly fill the pan. If your baking pan doesn't have a tight-fitting lid, place one long sheet of foil over another the same length. Fold over one long side by ½ inch (1 cm) and crimp tightly; fold and crimp another ½ inch. Open up the two sheets into one larger one and tightly crease the center seam. Cover the pan, crimping the edges tightly. This craftsmanship really helps preserve vital moisture in the meat.

Place the pan in the oven and lower the temperature to 300°F (150°C). Bake slowly until the meat is beautifully juicy, highly aromatic, and meltingly tender, about 2 hours. Remove the foil, turn on your broiler, and brown the ribs until the meat is deliciously glazed, about 10 minutes. At the table start trading ribs for favors. Pour any accumulated juices in the pan over the delicious ribs.

2 racks of baby back pork ribs
½ cup (125 mL) of honey
½ cup (125 mL) of yellow mustard
1 heaping tablespoon (18 mL) or so of dried thyme
½ teaspoon (2 mL) of salt

> **TWIST**
>
> This is a simple method for slowly baking ribs with any wet flavors, so you can freestyle lots of variations from your pantry. The honey can easily be replaced with maple syrup, brown sugar, any jam or jelly, or marmalade. The aromatic thyme can easily be swapped for any other fragrant herb or spice. And you have lots of interesting choices in the mustard department.

BACON ROAST PORK TENDERLOIN

Just when you thought you'd seen and tasted every bacon trick in the book, along comes an old-school classic to remind us how iconic bacon has always been. I was wrapping and roasting pork tenderloin with bacon as a menu staple twenty years ago. I'm glad this tasty method has stood the test of time. SERVES 2, EASILY DOUBLED

A large pork tenderloin

1 tablespoon (15 mL) of brown sugar

1 tablespoon (15 mL) of your
favorite mustard

1 teaspoon (5 mL) of your favorite
herb or spice, such as dried thyme,
minced fresh rosemary,
or cinnamon

½ teaspoon (2 mL) of salt

Lots of freshly cracked black pepper

3 to 4 slices of bacon

Preheat your oven to 500°F (260°C) and turn on your convection fan if you have one. Line a small baking sheet with parchment paper.

Prepare the pork tenderloin for roasting. Carefully slice away the tough white "silverskin" coating, leaving any visible fat in place. In a small bowl, whisk together the brown sugar, mustard, your preferred herb or spice, salt, and pepper. Rub this sauce all over the tenderloin, coating it thoroughly.

Fold several inches of the thin end of the tenderloin under itself to even out the meat's thickness. Wrap the bacon around the meat, beginning at the folded end, holding the bacon end tightly in place as you stretch the other around, overlapping it as you go. Secure the ends of the bacon with a short piece of dry spaghetti. This will dissolve and disappear as it cooks. Place the pork on the prepared baking sheet.

Roast the pork tenderloin until it reaches an internal temperature of 145°F (65°C), about 20 minutes. The intense heat of the oven renders and crisps the bacon and cooks the meat within. Let it rest for a few minutes, then slice, serve, and share!

------------------ TWIST ------------------
You can freestyle many flavorful rubs for the pork tenderloin before you seal on the bacon. Generally anything sweet can replace the brown sugar. Try any jam, jelly, or marmalade. Even good old barbecue sauce works well.

MUSTARD BACON STRIPS

A slice of simple bacon is a blank canvas, a masterpiece just waiting to happen, a treat in the works. So when you need a guaranteed crowd pleaser, an easily shared treat, or just some addictive crunch for your next sandwich, try this recipe. Slather aromatic sweetness over a pan full of bacon strips, crisp away, and you'll see how easy it is to satisfy a craving for grown-up bacon candy you didn't even know you had. **MAKES 12 TO 15 STRIPS OF DECADENT DELICIOUSNESS**

Preheat your oven to 350°F (180°C) and turn on your convection fan if you have one. To speed cleanup, line a baking sheet with parchment paper or a nonstick liner.

Stir the brown sugar and mustard into a smooth paste. Lay the bacon strips out on the prepared baking sheet, fitting them tightly together but not overlapping. Slather the mustard mixture evenly over the bacon. Sprinkle evenly with the cumin seeds. Finish with lots of freshly ground pepper.

Bake until the seasoned bacon strips are crispy and crunchy, 30 minutes or so. Keep an eye on the slices and let them get as crispy as you dare. Drain on paper towels and let cool. Serve on your favorite sandwich or in a salad, or chomp them down as soon as they're cool enough to handle!

½ cup (125 mL) of brown sugar

¼ cup (60 mL) of Dijon or your favorite mustard

1 pound (450 g) of thick-cut bacon

1 tablespoon (15 mL) or so of cumin or fennel seeds, or both

Lots of freshly ground pepper

TWIST

Bacon is pretty resilient and naturally friendly stuff. It can take just about any flavors you throw at it, so feel free to freestyle here. Try using just about any seed or other whole spice. Caraway seeds, chili powder, curry powder, poppy seeds, and almonds reward patient cooking and crisping. Brown sugar is delicious but so are honey, maple syrup, and molasses.

BACON WHISKEY JAM

This is a jar full of the most preposterous-sounding, implausibly flavored, yet deliciously addictive jam that will ever cross your lips. Bacon crisped and simmered with onions, brown sugar, and whiskey—smooth bacon heaven ready to spread on anything and everything. You might as well make a double batch now. You're going to need it. MAKES 2 CUPS (500 ML)

2 pounds (900 g) of thick-cut bacon, chopped

8 onions, chopped

2 cups (500 mL) of brown sugar

2 cups (500 mL) of water

2 cups (500 mL) of whiskey

1 teaspoon (5 mL) or so of red wine vinegar

Place your favorite large saucepan over medium-high heat. Toss in the bacon, then add a big splash of water. Stir frequently with a wooden spoon. As the water simmers, the bacon will begin to cook. Then, as the water evaporates, the bacon will render, releasing its fat. Lastly, it will crisp as the fat left behind heats past the boiling point of water into the browning and flavor zone. Adjust the heat as needed, keeping the bacon sizzling but not burning. Stir and be patient, until the bacon is evenly cooked and nicely browned but still slightly soft and not particularly crisp, about 20 minutes.

Remove the bacon bits and strain off all but ¼ cup (60 mL) or so of the drippings. Pile in the onions and patiently brown over lower and lower heat until they are soft, caramelized, and nicely browned, about 30 minutes. Return the bacon bits to the pan, accompanied by the brown sugar and water. Simmer until the water is absorbed and the mixture becomes thick and jam-like, another 20 minutes or so. Pour in the whiskey, reserving a shot or so for the finish, and cook until you get the works back to a thickened jam consistency, another 20 minutes.

Scrape the mixture into your food processor; splash in the vinegar and the reserved shot of whiskey. Pulse the works until smoother but still a bit chunky and rustic. Bacon heaven ready for serving and sharing!

TWIST

It took me a few tries to work out this jam recipe. Where there's a will there's a way! I figured I could simply crisp a lot of bacon, melt sugar into it, and purée smooth. It wasn't until I got there that I realized whiskey would be perfect in the mix. In my initial attempts, the bacon was too crisp and it stayed gritty in the jam. That's avoided in the final recipe. As you make a batch, imagine what steam-punk jam—or other dish—you might divine and fashion.

CURRIED LAMB SHANKS

This dish shows how spectacularly you can coax out the rich, meaty flavors of lamb shanks as you patiently braise and tenderize them. Big, bold flavor and silky, tender texture await the patient cook. Discover why so many chefs prefer lamb shanks above all other meats. SERVES 4, MAYBE 6 IF YOU'RE WILLING TO SHARE AND LOSE THE BONES

Position a rack toward the bottom of your oven so the lamb can cook evenly in the middle. Preheat the oven to its highest setting, 550° or 500°F (290° or 260°C), and turn on your convection fan and broiler if you have one.

Dry the lamb shanks with paper towels, then lightly rub them with oil. Arrange them neatly on a baking sheet or in a roasting pan. Roast, turning as needed, until browned all over, about 15 minutes. This step is not meant to cook the shanks through, but instead it's your only opportunity to add rich high-heat flavor to the meat's exterior before the simmering ahead. Remove the shanks from the oven and lower the temperature to 300°F (150°C).

Meanwhile, melt the butter in a large braising pot over medium-high heat. Add the onions and garlic; stir for a few minutes as the textures soften and flavors strengthen. Stir in the curry powder and cardamom. Then stir in the jalapeño (if using), ginger, and cumin seeds. Cook, stirring, for a minute or two. Nestle the browned shanks and any of their juices in the pot. Add the tomatoes, water, and salt. Bring to a full simmer, then cover with a tight-fitting lid and return the shanks to the oven. Braise until the meat transforms from tough to tender silkiness, 2 hours or so. Serve and share with lots of the flavorful sauce and heaps of cilantro scattered on top!

4 lamb shanks

A splash of vegetable oil

2 tablespoons (30 mL) of butter

4 onions, chopped

Cloves from 1 head of garlic, peeled

1 tablespoon (15 mL) of your favorite curry powder

1 tablespoon (15 mL) of ground cardamom

1 jalapeño pepper, seeded and chopped (optional)

A few inches (5 cm or so) of frozen ginger, grated

1 tablespoon (15 mL) of cumin seeds

A 28-ounce (796 mL) can of whole tomatoes

1 cup (250 mL) of water

A pinch of salt

A handful or two of fresh cilantro leaves and sprigs

TWIST

You can trust that with initial browning and patient simmering in aromatic liquid, lamb shanks will reliably tenderize and absorb whatever flavors you happen to surround them with. Try an apple cider theme with grainy mustard; Thai curry paste and coconut cream; barbecue spices; or just submerged in the first of a pair of bottles of really good red wine—with the second bottle, of course, reserved for drinking with the fragrant proceeds later on.

RED WINE BRAISED LAMB SHANKS

I braise with wine more than I do with broth or stock. Common in the classic kitchens of yore, forgotten yet craved in the driven kitchens of today, true meat broths and stocks are a rare commodity. When you have a few lamb shanks in need of immediate braising, it's much easier to procure a few cups of delicious red wine. That still leaves lots of room for aromatic flavors and hearty veggies, the basis and basics of this braising play. SERVES 4 TO 6

A splash of vegetable oil

4 lamb shanks

Cloves from 1 head of garlic, halved

12 shallots, peeled

2 carrots, peeled and cut into 3 or 4 chunks each

2 parsnips, peeled and cut into 3 or 4 chunks each

1 turnip, peeled and cut into 8 or 12 chunks

12 baby potatoes

1 bottle (750 mL) of your favorite big red wine

2 bay leaves

3 large sprigs of fresh rosemary

1 tablespoon (15 mL) of juniper berries

1 teaspoon (5 mL) of salt

Place a large Dutch oven or stew pot over medium-high heat, then splash in enough oil to coat the bottom with a thin film. Carefully add the lamb shanks to the hot oil and begin browning well on all sides. Be patient! This is the only opportunity you'll have to add the rich flavors of high-heat browning before the lower-heat simmering ahead.

When the shanks are evenly browned, pile in the garlic, shallots, carrots, parsnips, turnip, and potatoes. Add the wine along with the bay leaves, rosemary, juniper berries, and salt. Bring the works to a boil. Reduce the heat to a slow, steady simmer, cover, and continue cooking over low heat until the lamb shanks are very tender, about 2 hours. Poke them with a fork to be sure.

Place a shank in each serving bowl, spoon in lots of vegetables, and pour in steaming ladlefuls of the aromatic broth. Serve and share!

> **TWIST**
>
> A dish like this is a great opportunity to taste the relationship between the wines in your cooking and the wines in your glass. It's usually recommended that you drink the same wine you cook with. You'll soon notice how dramatically different the flavors of wines can be in cooking, where you're always rewarded for big, bold flavor. Save subtlety for the glass, though.

HERB-CRUSTED RACK OF LAMB

A neatly crusted rack of lamb is perhaps the most elegant cut of meat you can grace your table with. The delicate meat is both protected and flavored by the strongly aromatic crust, and the presentation is enhanced by the stunning crust. SERVES 2 TO 4

Preheat your oven to 375°F (190°C) and turn on your convection fan if you have one.

Pour a splash of vegetable oil into a large ovenproof skillet poised over medium-high heat. Season the lamb liberally with salt and pepper. Quickly sear the exposed lamb flesh until it's crusty and delicious on all sides. Remove from the pan and let cool slightly. Drain any excess fat from the pan.

In a small bowl, stir together the bread crumbs, garlic, herb of your choice, and olive oil, forming a crumbly paste. Thoroughly brush the meaty and fatty sides of the rack with mustard, then firmly pat the bread crumb mixture over the mustard.

Return the crusted lamb racks to the skillet with the crust side facing up and the bones down. Roast until the crust is lightly browned and the internal temperature reaches 130°F (55°C), signifying medium-rare, 20 minutes or so.

A big splash of vegetable oil

2 large racks of lamb, frenched

½ teaspoon (2 mL) of salt

Lots of freshly ground pepper

½ cup (125 mL) of fresh bread crumbs

2 cloves of garlic, finely minced

1 tablespoon (15 mL) of any minced fresh herb, such as thyme, sage, or rosemary

1 tablespoon (15 mL) of olive oil

¼ cup (60 mL) or so of Dijon mustard

TWIST

The bread crumbs in this classic method can easily be replaced with a variety of other savory toppings, including various semi-savory whole-grain cereals, oatmeal, potato flakes, ground flax seed, or one of my favorites, rye bread crumbs with extra caraway seeds.

FISH & SEAFOOD

BACON GARLIC SCAMPI WITH RED WINE MUSTARD SAUCE

"Scampi" sometimes means a type of shrimp, but more commonly it means a type of shrimp dish, usually with lots of garlic and wine. Every chef has a version of scampi up their sleeve ready to whip out when they need big flavor in a hurry. Here's mine, complete with a bit of tasty bacon to get the garlic party started. SERVES 4

8 slices of bacon, thinly sliced

1 pound (450 g) of penne or your favorite pasta

Cloves from 1 head of garlic, finely chopped

1 teaspoon (5 mL) of chili flakes

1 pound (450 g) of large shrimp, peeled

1 cup (250 mL) of your favorite red wine

1 tablespoon (15 mL) of Dijon mustard

Leaves from 1 bunch of fresh parsley, finely chopped

½ teaspoon (2 mL) of salt

Lots of freshly ground pepper

Bring a large pot of salted water to a boil for cooking the pasta.

Toss the bacon into your favorite medium saucepan over medium-high heat. Pour in a few splashes of water. Cook, stirring frequently, helping the water help the bacon cook, render, and crisp evenly. When the bacon is evenly browned and crisp, remove it with a slotted spoon, leaving behind the tasty bacon fat. Drain the bacon bits on paper towels. Now is the time to toss the pasta into the boiling water.

Add the garlic and chili flakes to the bacon fat and cook, stirring over medium-high heat, just long enough to release a heady garlic aroma, a minute or so. Toss in the shrimp, stirring until they turn bright orange, another few minutes. Add the wine and reduce for a minute to blend and concentrate the flavors. Complete the sauce by stirring in the mustard.

Meanwhile, cook then drain the pasta. Return it steaming hot to the pot, then add the bacon bits, shrimp mixture, and chopped parsley. Season with salt and lots of ground pepper. Stir together, serve, and share!

> ### TWIST
> Basic shrimp scampi is a dish of shrimp sautéed in garlic butter and finished with dry white wine. Beyond that, the rest is up to you. The dish is one of the most common menu items in North America and is thus subject to the whims of chefs everywhere. You can easily create your version to add to the canon. Just use lots of garlic and wine, stir in your own ideas, and make sure it tastes good!

SLOW-POACHED SHRIMP COCKTAIL

We're so used to shrimp being overcooked that we expect it to be rubbery and chewy, but it doesn't have to be that way. Locked inside your next purchase of shrimp is a revelation of tender texture that will change the way you think of North America's most popular seafood. Try this simple method that gently poaches the shrimp instead of vigorously boiling it. **SERVES 4**

Start with the cocktail sauce. Simply whisk together the ketchup, horseradish, soy sauce, Worcestershire, and lemon zest and juice. Refrigerate until needed.

For the poached shrimp, pour the water and wine into a large saucepan. Add the lemon zest and juice, onion, garlic, bay leaves, and salt. Bring to a full simmer over medium-high heat, then simmer for a few minutes to release flavors. Add the shrimp, stir, cover with a tight-fitting lid, turn off the heat, and let sit for exactly 10 minutes. Remove the shrimp, have a snack, and get to work peeling—or cool the works in the pan for delayed shrimp gratification. Serve, dip away, and share!

For the cocktail sauce
1 cup (250 mL) of ketchup, seafood sauce, or chili sauce

½ cup (125 mL) of prepared horseradish

1 tablespoon (15 mL) of soy sauce

1 tablespoon (15 mL) of Worcestershire sauce

The zest and juice of 1 lemon

For the poached shrimp
3 cups (750 mL) of water

1 cup (250 mL) of your favorite white wine

The zest and juice of 1 lemon

1 onion, thinly sliced

2 or 3 garlic cloves, thinly sliced

2 bay leaves

2 teaspoons (10 mL) of salt

1 pound (450 g) of extra-large shrimp (16–20 count), shells on, thawed but chilly

---
TWIST

Try a few freestyle flavor touches in the shrimp poaching liquid. All kinds of herbs and spices work well, so try your favorites—chili powder, curry powder, dill, oregano, even saffron. Use orange juice or more wine instead of water. And the cocktail sauce is ripe with opportunities too. With a base of a sharp horseradish edge and strong tomato flavor, you're free to improv the rest.

SAFFRON SHRIMP SHOTS

Shrimp cocktail is North America's most popular way to serve our most popular seafood. But doesn't every cocktail need a bit of booze to earn its stripes? They don't call it a cocktail party for nothing! These shrimp are all dressed up and ready for a night on the town. MAKES 12 FESTIVE SHOTS, WITH A FEW DELIGHTFUL LEFTOVER SHRIMP

Cocktail sauce (page 119)

Poached shrimp
(page 119—add 1 teaspoon/5 mL
    saffron to the poaching liquid)

For the shots
¼ cup (60 mL) of celery salt

Lemon wedge

12 fresh oysters (hopefully from
    Prince Edward Island)

1 cup (250 mL) or so of your favorite
    chilled vodka (I love Prince Edward
    Distillery's potato vodka)

For the shrimp garnishes
A sheet of nori seaweed sushi wrap

A handful of fresh chives

12 stuffed green cocktail olives

Craft and chill the cocktail sauce, then poach the shrimp. With the addition of the saffron to the poaching liquid, you'll be rewarded with golden shrimp as the saffron color emerges and soaks in. Remove the shrimp, discarding the poaching liquid.

Pour a small mound of celery salt onto a small plate. Dampen the rim of each of 12 shot glasses with a lemon wedge, then dip ½ inch (1 cm) or so of the glass into the celery salt. The aromatic powder will stick to the moist rim, garnishing the glass. Carefully shuck an oyster into each shot glass. Cover the oyster with a spoonful of cocktail sauce, leaving room for a splash of vodka.

Cut the nori wrap with scissors into long, thin strips, each about ½ inch (1 cm) wide by 3 or 4 inches (8 or 10 cm) long. Lay a single shrimp on your work surface so it curves toward you. Lay 2 long chives along the top of the shrimp. Wrap a nori strip around the middle of the shrimp so that it fits snugly like a belt and holds the chives in place. Fit an olive into the curve of the shrimp. Pierce the head end with a frilly toothpick or skewer, and poke it all the way through the olive and into the tail end of the shrimp. Repeat until you have 12 garnishes. Place each one atop a shot glass and serve and share with a flourish!

------------------------------ TWIST ------------------------------
This is not the sort of dish that should be taken too seriously. Indeed, the shot glass garnishes are really just an elaborate invitation for you to have fun decorating. Anything goes. Feel free to throw in any flairs and flourishes you can think of—they'll be right at home.

SAFFRON
SHRIMP
SHOTS

PAN-RUSHED SALMON WITH BACON CLAM CHOWDER

This is one of my favorite ways to cook salmon. The method is easy and infinitely variable, and the flavors are memorably hearty. Imagine a fillet of crispy salmon smothered with a quick, tasty chowder. Actually you don't have to imagine—just get cooking and have a taste! SERVES 4

Toss the bacon into your favorite large skillet. Pour in a few splashes of water. Stir frequently over medium-high heat, helping the water help the bacon cook, render, and crisp evenly. When the bacon is evenly browned and crisp, remove it with a slotted spoon, leaving the tasty bacon fat behind. Drain the bacon bits on paper towels.

Add the salmon fillets, skin side down, to the searing-hot bacon fat. Carefully sear each side until crusty and golden, turning carefully once, 2 to 3 minutes per side. Don't worry that the fish isn't cooked through; your goal here is just to add golden-brown crispy flavor. Transfer the salmon to a plate.

Add the onion, garlic, and celery to the pan; sauté as their textures soften and flavors strengthen, 5 minutes or so. Add the clams and their juice, the cream, sherry, and bay leaf; bring everything to a simmer. In a small bowl sprinkle the cornstarch into the water, then stir until smooth. Slowly pour the cornstarch slurry into the chowder, stirring constantly as the starch absorbs the moisture around it and thickens the chowder, just a minute or two more.

Nestle the salmon into the rich chowder. Cover with a tight-fitting lid, reduce the heat, and gently simmer until the fish is just cooked through, just 5 minutes more. Carefully transfer the salmon fillets to bowls. Stir the green onions and parsley into the chowder, then ladle it over the salmon. Sprinkle with the bacon bits. Serve and share!

4 slices of thick-cut bacon, chopped

4 large skin-on or skinless salmon fillets (about 6 ounces/170 g each)

1 onion, chopped

2 garlic cloves, minced

1 celery rib, chopped

A 5-ounce (142 g) can of clams

1 cup (250 mL) of whipping cream

¼ cup (60 mL) of your favorite sherry

1 bay leaf

1 teaspoon (5 mL) of cornstarch

¼ cup (60 mL) of water

2 green onions, chopped

2 tablespoons (30 mL) or so of chopped fresh parsley

TWIST

Sear, sauce, and simmer—the three steps of pan-rushing. This method is ideal for freestyling your own ideas, and the sauce step is the best place to stir them in. This recipe features a simple chowder, but the pan could just as easily be filled with any sauce that you like with seafood. While the seared salmon rests, you can take a moment and craft the special-of-the-day before simmering away to the finish.

PAN-RUSHED SALMON WITH THREE TOMATOES

Salmon's versatility is on full display in this dish. The fish is easy to cook and just as easy to pair with any sauce flavors you like. In this recipe, familiar tomatoes and oregano lead the way as you sear, sauce, and simmer your way to dinner. SERVES 4

A splash or two of vegetable oil

4 large skin-on or skinless salmon fillets (about 6 ounces/170 g each)

1 onion, chopped

4 garlic cloves, minced

1 cup (250 mL) or so of canned whole tomatoes

1 pint (500 mL) of cherry tomatoes, halved

½ cup (125 mL) of dried tomatoes

1 tablespoon (15 mL) of dried oregano

1 teaspoon (5 mL) of salt

A dash of pepper

¼ cup (60 mL) of chopped fresh oregano

Match a large skillet with a tight-fitting lid. Heat the skillet over medium-high heat and splash in enough oil to coat the bottom with a thin film. Carefully add the salmon fillets, skin side down, and sear until lightly browned on each side, turning carefully once, 3 or 4 minutes per side. Don't worry that the fish isn't cooked through; your goal is just to add golden-brown crispy flavor. Transfer the salmon to a plate.

Add the onion and garlic to the pan; lightly sauté for 2 to 3 minutes, awakening their flavors. Add the whole tomatoes, crushing them by hand as you go. Add the cherry tomatoes, dried tomatoes, dried oregano, salt, and pepper. Bring the works to a simmer and cook gently, softening textures and strengthening flavors, 2 or 3 minutes. Reduce the heat to a low simmer.

Carefully nestle the salmon fillets into the gently simmering sauce. Cover tightly and simmer until the salmon is cooked through, 4 to 5 minutes. Plate the salmon, ladle on the sauce, and garnish with lots of chopped oregano. Serve and share!

---------- TWIST ----------
I love the fresh, intense flavor of true sun-ripened tomatoes in any dish—which is why this dish doesn't include any. Ripe local tomatoes are a once-a-year indulgence, but the rest of the year you can come close to capturing their true flavor with a combination of three other tomatoes: canned for sunny flavor, cherry for fresh texture, and dried for depth of flavor. Together, these three make an excellent tomato team ready to spark many other dishes.

SALMON IN A BAG

French cooking includes a basic method for steaming fish with vegetables and aromatics inside tightly folded parchment paper. Known as *en papillote*, this classic method efficiently locks in heat and flavors. It's speedy—and it's even speedier if you use the parchment cooking bags that can be found in grocery stores now. (For best results, look for Parchment Cooking Bags from PaperChef.) SERVES 4

Preheat your oven to 350°F (180°C) and turn on your convection fan if you have one.

In a large bowl, toss the fennel with the olives, tomatoes, oil, vinegar, fennel seeds, salt, and pepper. Evenly divide the works among 4 parchment cooking bags.

Lightly season each salmon fillet with a bit more salt and pepper. Lay the bags on their side and slip a salmon fillet into each one, surrounding it with the pile of aromatic vegetables. Tightly roll or fold up the open end until you get to the salmon, then use a binder clip, clothespin, or stapler to seal the bag, creating a pocket of moist heat and flavor. Transfer the bags to a baking sheet.

Bake for about 20 minutes, until the bags heat through and puff up with aromatic steam, cooking the fish within. Remove from the oven and place each bag on a plate. Encourage everyone at your table to cut open their own bag, thereby releasing a cloud of fragrant steam. Serve and share!

1 fennel bulb, very thinly sliced

1 cup (250 mL) of your favorite pitted black olives

A heaping ½ cup (140 mL) of drained oil-packed dried tomatoes, thinly sliced

¼ cup (60 mL) of extra-virgin olive oil

¼ cup (60 mL) of red wine vinegar

2 tablespoons (30 mL) of fennel seeds

½ teaspoon (2 mL) of salt

Lots of freshly ground pepper

4 large skinless salmon fillets (about 6 ounces/170 g each)

- - - - - - - - - - - - - **TWIST** - - - - - - - - - - - - -

This basic method of locking salmon, vegetables, and fragrant moisture into a bag can easily be adapted with many other flavor themes. For a bag of Indian-inspired flavor, toss thinly sliced fennel with curry powder, orange juice, and mango chutney. For Asian flair, toss thinly sliced shiitake mushrooms, onions, and snow peas with rice wine vinegar, soy sauce, and grated ginger.

PAN-SEARED SCALLOPS WITH TOMATO CAPER RELISH

The mild, delicate flavor of scallops can be enjoyed many different ways, but my favorite is simply seared golden brown and crispy delicious. This versatile method adds rich flavor and addictive texture that's perfectly complemented by any quick, bright sauce or condiment. SERVES 4

1 pound (450 g) of large fresh
   sea scallops

A splash or two of canola oil

½ pint (250 mL) of cherry tomatoes

2 green onions, sliced

1 tablespoon (15 mL) of capers, drained

The zest and juice of ½ lemon

¼ teaspoon (1 mL) of salt

Lots of freshly ground pepper

Heat your favorite large, heavy skillet over high heat. While the pan is heating, dry the scallops between layers of paper towel. Remove the small, tough fibrous muscle on their side. (The big white scallop is the muscle that this filter feeder uses to open and close its shell. The much smaller side muscle is used to lock the shell tightly shut, which is why it's so tough and should be discarded.)

Pour enough oil into the hot pan to coat the bottom with a thin film. Carefully and quickly position the scallops in the oil. Sear them, turning once, until they're golden brown and crusty on the outside but still tender inside, just 1 or 2 minutes per side. Transfer the scallops to a plate and loosely tent with foil to keep warm.

Add the cherry tomatoes, green onions, capers, lemon zest and juice, salt, and pepper to the searing-hot pan. Toss together until heated through and well mixed, just another minute or so. Serve and share the seared scallops with the warm relish.

------------------------------ TWIST ------------------------------
The secret to this basic method is a preheated heavy pan that won't cool when the scallops are added. It's vitally important that the pan stay searing hot in the first few minutes of cooking. If not, the scallops will just release moisture and dry out without really gaining any seared flavor. Once you master this method, you'll easily be able to craft a sauce or two of your own. Any quick, bright flavors will do.

PAN-FRIED CRISPY CRUSTY WHITEFISH

This is a deceptively simple way to cook just about any type of white-fleshed fish fillets: dipped in egg and simply crusted with seasoned flour, then crisply pan-fried in browned butter. Sometimes all it takes is a crispy crust to inspire a fish feeding frenzy at your table! **SERVES 4 TO 6**

Heat your favorite large skillet over medium-high heat.

In a large shallow dish, stir together the flour, herb or spice, salt, and pepper. In a second shallow dish, vigorously whisk the eggs. One at a time, dip the fish fillets into the seasoned flour, thoroughly coating them and gently shaking off any excess. Next dip the fillets into the eggs, again coating them thoroughly and carefully draining off any extra. Lastly, dredge them through the flour yet again. Transfer to a sheet of waxed paper.

Pour a small splash of oil into the hot pan. Working quickly, place the butter in the middle of the insulating oil and gently swirl the works as the butter quickly melts, froths, and browns. Immediately add the fish fillets to the pan. Sizzle and sear each side, turning once, until crispy, golden brown, and delicious, 2 or 3 minutes per side. Serve and share!

2 cups (500 mL) of any flour

¼ cup (60 mL) of dried dill, dried tarragon, curry powder, chili powder, Old Bay Seasoning, or your favorite dried herb or spice

1 teaspoon (5 mL) of salt

Lots of freshly ground pepper

4 eggs

4 fresh skinless haddock fillets (5 to 6 ounces/140 to 170 g each), or any other white fish such as hake, halibut, cod, tilapia, or sole

A splash of any vegetable oil

2 or 3 tablespoons (30 to 45 mL) of butter

- - - - - - - - - - - - - - TWIST - - - - - - - - - - - - - -

This basic crusting method is easy to experiment with. For example, I often use whole wheat flour for a bit more crunch and a tasty appearance. Any herb or spice works well, but I really like Old Bay, a traditional Maritime seasoning.

BOTTOMLESS POT
OF STEAMED MUSSELS

Mussels are the easiest seafood to cook. You can just pour them into a covered pot with nothing else and in a few minutes they'll steam and release lots of their addictively flavorful broth. It's that easy! But it's just as easy to add a few aromatic flavor twists and freestyle your own version of this tasty seafood treat. You'll never run out of ideas or mussels again! SERVES 2 TO 4

For the soak-up bread

1 baguette or any loaf of bread

¼ cup (60 mL) or so of olive oil

For the mussels

2 tablespoons (30 mL) of butter, vegetable oil, olive oil, or bacon fat

2 onions, chopped

4 or more garlic cloves, minced

1 heaping tablespoon (18 mL) of chopped fresh or dried dill or your favorite herb or spice

1 cup (250 mL) of your favorite white wine, red wine, full-flavored beer, or juice or tomato sauce

5 pounds (2.25 kg) of fresh mussels

Begin with the soak-up bread. Preheat your oven to 400°F (200°C) and turn on your convection fan if you have one. Thinly slice the baguette on the diagonal and neatly arrange the slices on a baking sheet. Brush each slice liberally with olive oil. Bake until thoroughly crisp and golden brown all over, about 10 minutes. Be patient and let every piece get the browning treatment. Set aside.

Move on to the mussels. Match a large pot with a tight-fitting lid. Over medium heat, melt the butter, then toss in the onions and garlic, sautéing until golden and fragrant, a few minutes. Add the dill and white wine. Bring the works to a quick simmer, then pile in the mussels. Cover and continue cooking, steaming the mussels so they open their shells and release their broth, about 10 minutes. The mussels are done when all the shells have opened. Discard any unopened ones.

Divvy up the mussels among your serving bowls, pour the juices evenly over them, and pass around the soak-up bread. Serve and share!

---- TWIST ----

Use this recipe as a jumping-off point to experiment with your own ideas. Just make roughly equal substitutions and see what you can create. Perhaps a great place to start is with a few slices of crisped bacon and a bottle of your favorite ale.

MEDITERRANEAN FISH STEW

If you live near the sea, chances are you have some kind of local fish stew tradition. This one is inspired by the flavors of the Mediterranean, but not by a quest for authenticity. If you crave the real thing, get on a plane. If you're looking for a delicious, aromatic dish, stay here! **SERVES 4 TO 6**

Pour the olive oil into your favorite large soup pot over medium-high heat. Toss in the onion, garlic, and fennel; sauté, softening the textures and strengthening the flavors, 3 or 4 minutes. Add the tomatoes, breaking them up into smaller pieces by hand. Add the orange zest and juice, fennel seeds, coriander seeds, saffron, salt, and pepper. Bring to a slow, steady simmer, then stir in the fish. Continue to simmer until the fish is cooked through, maybe 5 minutes more. Stir in the green onions at the last second. Ladle the stew into festive bowls and drizzle each at the table with a spoonful of anise liqueur. Serve and share!

¼ cup (60 mL) of your very best extra-virgin olive oil

1 onion, diced

4 garlic cloves, minced

1 fennel bulb, diced

A 28-ounce (796 mL) can of whole tomatoes

The zest and juice of 4 oranges

1 tablespoon (15 mL) of fennel seeds

1 tablespoon (15 mL) of coriander seeds

¼ teaspoon (1 mL) of saffron

½ teaspoon (2 mL) of salt

Lots of freshly ground pepper

1 to 2 pounds (450 to 900 g) of your favorite mixed fresh seafood or skinless fish, cut into 2- or 3-inch (5 or 8 cm) chunks

4 green onions, thinly sliced

¼ cup (60 mL) or so of anise liqueur, such as sambuca, Pernod, or ouzo

- - - - - - - - - - - - - - - TWIST - - - - - - - - - - - - - - -

In the spirit of fish stews everywhere, anything goes here. It's easy to get bogged down by talk of authenticity, but really, whatever seafood you can find is perfect for this stew.

TOMATO BASIL CRUSTED WHITEFISH

A tasty, crispy crust is an easy way to get any fish on the table. This particular topping is full of classic tomato basil flavor, but you can easily modify it to use whatever you have on hand. Either way, you'll be happy to see your table downing fish and drowning the chef with compliments! SERVES 4 TO 6

1 cup (250 mL) of any dried bread crumbs

½ cup (125 mL) of oil-packed dried tomatoes, drained

¼ cup (60 mL) of your best extra-virgin olive oil

Leaves from 1 bunch of fresh basil

4 fresh skinless haddock fillets (6 ounces/170 g or so each), or any other white-fleshed fish such as hake, halibut, cod, tilapia, or sole

½ teaspoon (2 mL) of salt

Lots of freshly ground pepper

Preheat your oven to 375°F (190°C) and turn on your convection fan if you have one. Line a small baking sheet with parchment paper.

Pile the bread crumbs, tomatoes, and olive oil into your food processor. Pulse a few times until the mixture becomes a paste of sorts. Add the fresh basil and pulse a few more times until the fragrant leaves are thoroughly chopped and mixed into the crust.

Neatly arrange the fish fillets on a small baking sheet so they touch each other. Lightly season their tops with salt and pepper. Divide the crust evenly among the fillets, pressing firmly and forming an even layer that completely covers the fish. Bake until the fish is cooked through and aromatic, 15 minutes or so. Serve and share!

TWIST

Instead of plain bread crumbs, try extra-crispy panko or small chunks of your favorite fresh bread. Substitute black olives, artichokes, or sautéed onions for the tomatoes. You can replace the fresh basil leaves with any fresh tender herb leaves—parsley, tarragon, or dill are nice—or a few spoonfuls of pesto or tapenade.

KETCHUP SALMON WITH ASIAN FLAVORS

I am an expert at persuading kids and finicky adults to eat salmon. I've tried every method and recipe known to mankind, even invented a few of my own. I have to admit, though, that nothing works better than ketchup. SERVES 4

Build a hardwood fire and let it die down to a thick bed of glowing coals, or prepare and preheat your barbecue or grill to its highest setting. Alternatively, preheat your oven to 375°F (190°C).

In a large resealable plastic bag, combine the ketchup, brown sugar, ginger, soy sauce, and salt. Mix the works well into a tasty marinade. Add the salmon, seal the bag, and gently massage, evenly coating the fish with the sauce. You can cook the salmon right away, but if you have the time, marinate the fish for a few hours or even overnight.

Grill or roast the salmon, turning once, until crispy and aromatic, about 5 minutes or so per side. Serve and share!

½ cup (125 mL) of ketchup

½ cup (125 mL) of brown sugar

2 or 3 inches (5 or 8 cm) of frozen ginger, grated

2 tablespoons (30 mL) of soy sauce

½ teaspoon (2 mL) of salt

4 large skin-on or skinless salmon fillets (6 ounces/170 g or so each)

TWIST

Replace the Asian flavors here with the flavor theme of your choice. Ketchup will easily embrace southwestern, Mediterranean, Indian, French, and even Moroccan flavors.

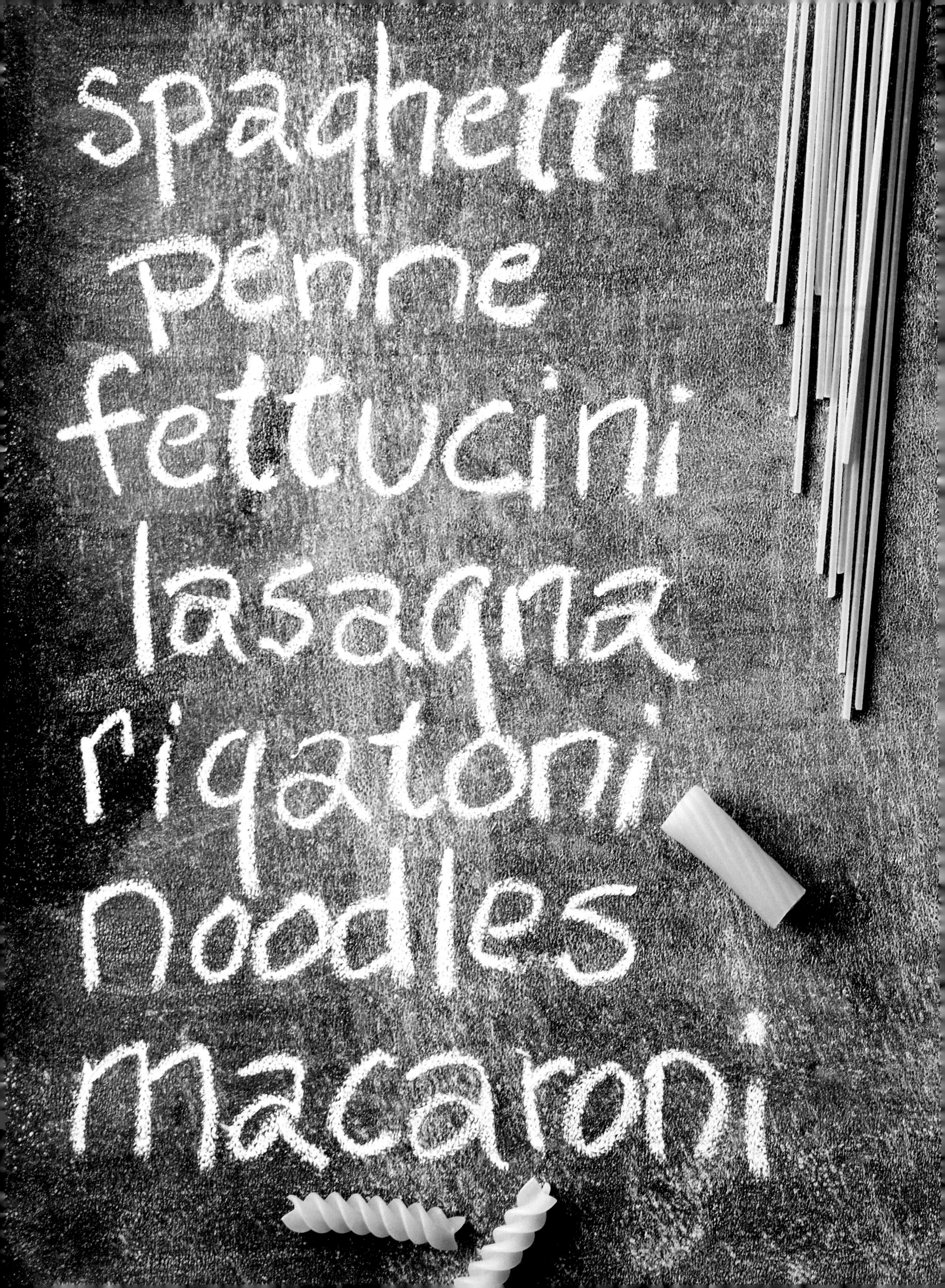

spaghetti

penne

fettucini

lasagna

rigatoni

noodles

macaroni

PASTA

SPAGHETTI WITH HOMEMADE TOMATO SAUCE

This is perhaps the most basic recipe of all, an essential part of every kitchen's repertoire. Here, though, the aim is to launch your own improv project. There's no shame in a bowl of basic tomato sauce with noodles—especially when you craft that sauce yourself—but with practice and a little everyday vision, you can stir in some freestyling too. Indulge your creativity a bit. Do ya good! By the way, don't turn your nose up at canned tomatoes. They'll give you the truest sunniest field-ripe flavor. SERVES 4 TO 6

2 tablespoons (30 mL) of extra-virgin olive oil or any vegetable oil

1 large onion, diced

Cloves from 1 head of garlic, minced

A 28-ounce (796 mL) can of diced, whole, or crushed tomatoes

1 heaping teaspoon (6 mL) of dried oregano or thyme

½ teaspoon (2 mL) of salt

Lots of freshly ground pepper

1 pound (450 g) of spaghetti

You can make this whole meal in the time it takes to boil the water and cook the spaghetti. You can even pick up a few pasta secrets along the way.

Begin by filling your largest pot with lots of the hottest water you can get from your tap. Set the pot over high heat and add salt. Taste the water: it should remind you of a fresh day at the beach. When the water is properly salted, as the pasta cooks it will absorb the seasoned water and in turn be seasoned. As you wait for the water to come to a boil, get started on the sauce.

Heat your favorite large skillet or saucepan over medium-high heat. Splash in the olive oil, then add the onion and garlic. Sauté until the textures soften and the flavors brighten, a few minutes of stirring and tossing. Pour in the tomatoes, then season the works with oregano, salt, and pepper. Bring the sauce to a boil, then lower the heat to a slow, steady simmer. Turn your attention back to your noodles.

Continued

- BOIL WATER
- MAKE SAUCE
- COOK PASTA

Once the water reaches a furious boil, add the spaghetti. Stir it frequently but don't watch the clock—watch the pasta. As it softens, keep an eye on its texture, fishing out and taste-testing as you go. (Sacrificial noodles for the greater good.) Cook the pasta until it's al dente, those magical moments when its texture has softened enough to enjoy but it's still deliciously chewy. Pasta is at its best with lots of texture—not soft but not too firm.

Drain the pasta well and don't rinse—you'll only wash away surface starches that help your fresh sauce adhere. Divide evenly among plates and ladle on the sauce. Serve and share!

TWIST

Jump out of the rut of using your favorite pasta and try new ones—a different noodle really changes this dish. As you craft the sauce, you'll also have lots of opportunity to stir in your own ideas. Start with the oil. For added flavor, fry and crisp a few slices of prosciutto or pancetta in it. You can even skip the oil altogether and fry up a few slices of hearty bacon, then use the bacon and its fat in the sauce. Use more or less garlic. Add a shredded carrot along with the other aromatic vegetables. Stir in chunks of chopped anything, any flavor at all from your fridge or kitchen shelves. A can of well-rinsed beans or chickpeas. Other tomatoes, fresh or dried. Spoonfuls of Mediterranean condiments such as tapenade or pesto. Fresh herbs—and lots of them—are the best for bright finishing flavor. Basil, of course, but fresh, never dried. Whole bunches of fresh basil leaves coarsely torn into the works is a revelation of flavor. Tarragon, chives, thyme, dill, parsley, green onions, oregano, rosemary, sage, and lovage all add freestyle flair.

PASTA WITH ROASTED TOMATOES, BELL PEPPERS & GOAT CHEESE

There's more than one way to get pasta and tomatoes to the table. Add a medley of sweet bell peppers, savory onions, fragrant garlic, the power of patient roasting, and the signature richness of soft goat cheese. This recipe is a reliable path to a bright pasta layered with deep, soulful flavor. SERVES 4 TO 6

8 ripe Roma tomatoes, halved lengthwise

1 each green, red, and yellow bell peppers, each cut into 8 chunks

Cloves from 1 head of garlic, halved

2 onions, peeled and cut in 8 wedges

¼ cup (60 mL) of extra-virgin olive oil

1 teaspoon (5 mL) of salt

Lots of freshly ground pepper

1 pound (450 g) of your favorite pasta

A 5-ounce (140 g) log of soft goat cheese, at room temperature

3 or 4 tablespoons (45 to 60 mL) of chopped fresh thyme (about 1 bunch)

Preheat your oven to 375°F (190°C) and turn on your convection fan if you have one.

Load a large roasting pan with the tomatoes, peppers, garlic, onions, olive oil, salt, and pepper. Toss the works gently with your fingers, evenly distributing the ingredients. Bake until you need to eat, 30 minutes or so. Better yet, be patient and wait, keeping an eye on the proceeds until a long, slow roasting releases a pan stew of epic proportions.

Once you like what you see in the oven, bring a large pot of salted water to a boil. Commit the pasta to the pot and cook until al dente. (For further insight, see pages 144 and 147.) Drain the hot, steamy pasta, but let it stay a bit moist—not soupy, just wet.

Return the pasta to the pot and immediately crumble in the soft goat cheese. Stir it vigorously, forming an improvised sauce of sorts for the moist, starchy pasta. Add the roasted vegetables, scraping all the goodness from the pan. Sprinkle with the pile of fresh thyme at the last minute, thus preserving its aromatic but delicate goodness for its finishing strength. Serve and share!

> **TWIST**
>
> Have a look at the recipe for spaghetti with tomato sauce on pages 144 and 147 for some quick insight into the pasta path. Great cooking—and pasta in particular—celebrates attention to detail. It's miraculous, really, how dried pasta can boil so vigorously in salted water, softening so dramatically yet holding on to so much texture and seasoning—enough to anchor all the great pasta dishes of the world.

PENNE PRIMAVERA WITH BASIL BOURSIN SAUCE

Primavera. Spring . . . first green. This classic New World pasta is founded on the simple principle that when you toss together steaming-hot pasta, a creamy cheese sauce, and lots of bright green vegetables, the result will be delicious. Especially when you twist in the tang of Boursin cheese and loads of fresh basil. SERVES 4 TO 6, EVEN 8 DEPENDING WHAT ELSE YOU STIR IN

Fill your largest pot with lots of hot water and lots of salt and put it over lots of heat. Bring the works to a boil. Review the pasta insights on pages 144 and 147.

Begin the sauce while you wait. Melt the butter in your favorite large saucepan over medium-high heat, then sauté the onion and garlic until their textures soften and the flavors brighten, no more than 5 minutes. Lower the heat and sprinkle the flour and nutmeg over the onions. Stir well until the flour is smoothly absorbed by the fat. Pour in the milk, raise the heat, and begin stirring gently with a wooden spoon. Season with salt and hot sauce. Simmer and stir. As the milk heats it will absorb the flour, and in turn the flour will swell and absorb the milk, thickening the works into a smooth sauce, in 5 minutes or so. Gently stir in the Boursin cheese until it has melted into the sauce. Remove from the heat and keep warm.

Fire the pasta, then the vegetables. Stir the pasta into the boiling water and wait 6 minutes. Toss in the broccoli, asparagus, and peas. Continue cooking until the vegetables are tender and green and the pasta is al dente, another 5 minutes or so. Drain the works and return everything to the pot. Pour in the cheese sauce, then add the basil and green onions at the last second, preserving their fragile, aromatic brightness. Gently stir the works together. Serve and share!

2 tablespoons (30 mL) of butter

1 large onion, diced

4 garlic cloves, minced

3 tablespoons (45 mL) of all-purpose flour

½ teaspoon (2 mL) of nutmeg

1 cup (250 mL) of milk

½ teaspoon (2 mL) of salt

¼ teaspoon (1 mL) of hot sauce

A 5-ounce (150 g) package of Boursin cheese

1 pound (450 g) of penne or your favorite pasta

1 bunch of broccoli, cut in small florets

1 bunch of asparagus, trimmed and cut in 2-inch (5 cm) pieces

1 cup (250 mL) of frozen peas

Leaves and tender stems from 1 bunch of fresh basil, thinly sliced

4 or 5 green onions, thinly sliced

TWIST

Pasta primavera remains a very popular menu item in the world of casual restaurants because it's easy to make and easy to stir just about anything in the kitchen into the works and dress it up for the Chef's Daily Special. Various fresh vegetables, herbs, and greens are fair game, as are a variety of fresh fish, even crisp bacon, and my favorite: a shredded rotisserie chicken.

FETTUCCINE ALFREDO WITH ASPARAGUS, TARRAGON & PINE NUTS

Pasta tossed with butter and cheese—inherently simple yet absolutely delicious. The essence of a classic. Good as is. Great updated as you wish, or here with asparagus, pine nuts, and sharp, bright tarragon. SERVES 4 TO 6

¼ cup (60 mL) of butter

2 garlic cloves, minced

1 cup (250 mL) of pine nuts

1 cup (250 mL) of whipping cream

1 pound (450 g) of fettuccine or tagliatelle

2 bunches of asparagus, trimmed

2 cups (500 mL) of fresh or frozen peas

1 heaping cup (275 mL) of grated true Parmigiano-Reggiano

Leaves from 1 bunch of fresh tarragon or basil

Lots of freshly ground pepper

Fill your largest pot with lots of hot water and lots of salt and put it over lots of heat. Bring the works to a boil. Review the pasta insights on pages 144 and 147.

Begin the sauce while you wait. Melt the butter in your favorite medium saucepan over medium-high heat until sizzling, then add the garlic and pine nuts, gently stirring them for a few minutes, toasting and flavoring them. Pour in the cream, raise the heat, and begin stirring gently with a wooden spoon. Simmer and stir. As the cream cooks it will reduce and thicken into a smooth sauce, in 5 minutes or so.

Fire the pasta, then the vegetables. Stir the pasta into the boiling water and wait 8 minutes. Toss in the asparagus and peas. Continue cooking until the vegetables are tender and bright green and the pasta is al dente, another 3 minutes or so. Drain the works and return everything to the pot. Pour in the butter sauce, add the grated cheese, and sprinkle on the tarragon leaves. Season generously with pepper. Gently stir everything together. Serve and share!

> **TWIST**
>
> Feel free to freestyle a few ideas into the midst of this simple pasta dish. You can splash in the wine or spirit of your choice and reduce it down with the cream. Pine nuts are neither classic nor essential. The asparagus role can be played by just about every single green vegetable. And any fresh herb is welcome too—just use lots!

TOMATO BASIL CARBONARA

The basic method that transforms steaming-hot noodles, simple eggs, and savory cheese into rich pasta carbonara is inherently flexible and inviting of frequent freestyle flourishes. In this version, the classic pairing of bright tomato and fresh basil shines yet again. SERVES 4 TO 6

Fill your largest pot with lots of hot water and lots of salt and put it over lots of heat. Bring the works to a boil. Review the pasta insights on pages 144 and 147.

Begin the sauce while you wait. In a medium bowl, whisk together the eggs, cheese, salt, and pepper. Set aside.

Splash the olive oil into your favorite small saucepan over medium-high heat and stir in the garlic. Cook, stirring, until the garlic is sizzling hot and fragrant, just 2 or 3 minutes. Turn off the heat and set aside.

Stir the pasta into the boiling water and cook until it's al dente, in 10 or 11 minutes or so. Drain the hot, steamy pasta, leaving it moist—not soupy, just wet—saving ¼ cup (60 mL) or so of the starchy cooking water. Return the pasta and the reserved cooking water to the pot. Working quickly—while the noodles are hottest—stir in the garlicky oil and the egg mixture, forming a thick, rich sauce as the eggs and hot moisture combine with the cheese.

At the last second, stir in the cherry tomatoes and basil leaves, preserving their fragile, aromatic brightness. Divvy up among pasta bowls. Serve and share!

3 eggs

1 cup (250 mL) of the very best grated Parmigiano-Reggiano cheese

½ teaspoon (2 mL) of salt

Lots of freshly ground pepper

2 tablespoons (30 mL) of extra-virgin olive oil

4 garlic cloves, minced

1 pound (450 g) of fettuccine

1 pint (500 mL) of cherry tomatoes, halved

Leaves and tender stems from 2 bunches of fresh basil, thinly sliced

---

TWIST

See what you can invent. Whisk the eggs and cheese together, sizzle the olive oil and garlic, cook the pasta. Stir together with your choice of a few final flavor flourishes. Fresh cherry tomatoes and basil. Roasted tomatoes and pesto. Roasted tomatoes and tapenade. Olives and chickpeas. Fennel and fennel seeds. Your table. Your kitchen. Your call!

PENNE WITH BABY SPINACH PESTO

Green is delicious. Green is healthy. And green is easy. This pasta shows off an exceptional pesto made with tender spinach leaves, then melted into steaming-hot noodles. It's tasty, vibrant, and spectacular! SERVES 4 TO 6

1 cup (250 mL) of pine nuts

¼ cup (60 mL) of your very best extra-virgin olive oil

½ teaspoon (2 mL) of salt

2 garlic cloves, peeled

1 cup (250 mL) of grated Parmigiano-Reggiano

5 ounces (140 g) of fresh baby spinach

1 pound (450 g) of penne

Fill your largest pot with lots of hot water and lots of salt and put it over lots of heat. Bring the works to a boil. Review the pasta insights on pages 144 and 147.

Make the pesto while you wait. In your food processor, combine the pine nuts, olive oil, salt, and garlic cloves. Pulse the works, neatly chopping the garlic to evenly distribute its flavors. Add the cheese and pulse smooth yet again. Cram in as much spinach as you can and process until it too grinds into the pesto. Repeat with any remaining spinach.

Fire the pasta and cook it until it's al dente, in 10 or 11 minutes or so. Drain the hot, steamy noodles, leaving them moist—not soupy, just wet—saving ½ cup (125 mL) or so of the starchy cooking water. Return the pasta and the reserved cooking water to the pot. Working quickly—while the noodles are hottest—stir all the pesto into the works. Serve and share immediately!

TWIST

Pestos are just flavorful pastes, so they're easily crafted from a wide variety of ingredients. They're best when they combine a fresh green herb, savory Parmesan cheese, olive oil, puréed nuts, and sharp, aromatic garlic. Beyond that, just fill in the blanks. Pestos are great for freestyling. You can use sage, goat cheese, and walnuts, or mint, Boursin, and pistachios. Or try cilantro, Cheddar, and pine nuts.

LOBSTER LASAGNA DI CARNEVALE

This dish is a big affair, but with tight planning and spirited execution, the results will be spectacular. If it's not a special occasion, this lasagna will instantly make it one. It's one of the world's great food rituals, an elaborate feast before famine. The send-off meal before Lent. A family's last chance to splurge in the kitchen with every possible indulgence crammed into one dish, even tiny, delicious meatballs. SERVES 8

Position a rack toward the bottom of the oven so the lasagna can bake evenly in the middle. Preheat the oven to 400°F (200°C) and turn on your convection fan if you have one. Lightly oil a large baking pan and a baking sheet.

Begin with the meatballs. In a medium bowl, combine the sausage meat, egg, bread crumbs, fennel seeds, mustard, and salt. Using your hands, gently and thoroughly mix the works together, evenly distributing the flavors. Roll up grape-size pieces and arrange on the baking sheet. Bake until lightly browned and cooked through, about 10 minutes. Remove and set aside. Lower the temperature to 375°F (190°C).

Next make the tomato sauce. Splash the olive oil into your favorite large saucepan over medium-high heat. Add the pancetta and prosciutto; sauté until lightly browned and crispy, about 3 minutes. Toss in the onion, garlic, and carrot; continue cooking as the textures soften and the flavors brighten, another 2 to 3 minutes. Stir in the tomatoes, tomato juice, red wine, and thyme. Cook a few minutes longer. Set aside.

For the cheese sauce, in a medium bowl, whisk the egg. Add the lobster, mozzarella, mascarpone, ricotta, Parmesan, and basil.

Continued

For the meatballs

3 Italian sausages, casings removed

1 egg, lightly whisked

½ cup (125 mL) of dry bread crumbs

1 tablespoon (15 mL) of fennel seeds

1 tablespoon (15 mL) of grainy mustard

½ teaspoon (2 mL) of salt

For the tomato sauce

A splash of extra-virgin olive oil

4 ounces (115 g) of pancetta, cubed

4 ounces (115 g) of thinly sliced prosciutto, rolled and sliced

1 onion, diced

Cloves from 1 head of garlic, chopped

1 carrot, grated

A 28-ounce (796 mL) can of whole tomatoes, preferably no-salt-added

1 cup (250 mL) of tomato juice

1 cup (250 mL) of your favorite red wine

2 teaspoons (10 mL) of dried thyme

For the cheese sauce

1 egg

2 cups (500 mL) of cooked lobster meat

2 cups (500 mL) of shredded mozzarella cheese

1 cup (250 mL) of mascarpone cheese

1 cup (250 mL) of ricotta cheese

1 cup (250 mL) of grated Parmesan cheese

Leaves from 1 bunch of fresh basil, coarsely chopped

For the topping

2 cups (500 mL) of shredded
   mozzarella cheese

1 cup (250 mL) of grated
   Parmesan cheese

7 ounces (200 g) of bocconcini cheese

A few sprigs of fresh thyme

For assembly

4 ounces (115 g) of thinly
   sliced prosciutto

1½ pounds (675 g) of no-boil
   lasagna noodles

For the topping, in a medium bowl, toss together the mozzarella and Parmesan.

Build the ultimate lasagna in a 14- × 10- × 3-inch (4 L) baking pan. Work in this order, taking the time to fit the noodles carefully into the pan, breaking a few into smaller sections to fill gaps:

- one-third of the tomato sauce
- one-third of the noodles
- one-third of the tomato sauce
- all the meatballs
- one-third of the noodles
- all the cheese sauce
- all the prosciutto slices, slightly overlapping
- the remaining noodles
- the remaining tomato sauce
- the mixed cheese topping
- the bocconcini

Artfully arrange a few thyme sprigs on top, just for looks.

Place one long sheet of foil over another the same length. Fold over one long side by ½ inch (1 cm) and crimp tightly; fold and crimp another ½ inch. Open up the two sheets into one larger one and tightly crease the center seam. Lightly oil one side and invert over the pan, covering it fully and crimping the edges tightly. This craftsmanship will help preserve vital moisture in the lasagna. Bake until all the layers have heated through and the noodles have tenderized, about 45 minutes. Remove the foil and bake for another 15 minutes, allowing the cheese topping to lightly brown. Let rest for a few minutes before slicing. Serve and share!

TWIST

Within this memorable lasagna are the essential components of the basic dish: noodles, tomato sauce, and cheese sauce. Together they form a firm foundation for mixing in the extravagance of lobster, meatballs, prosciutto, mascarpone, and bocconcini. This dish shows how easy it is to begin with a basic idea and stir in lots of twists and turns in the name of experimentation—and extravagance!

---

spaghetti
penne
fettucini
lasagna
rigatoni
noodles
macaroni

SPINACH LASAGNA

Lasagna is one of the world's great party dishes. Its spectacular flavors and presentation reward the intrepid cook, even when crafting this meatless, non-dairy, gluten-free version and packing the works with spinach. SERVES 8 TO 10

Position a rack toward the bottom of your oven so the lasagna can bake evenly in the middle. Preheat the oven to 375°F (190°C) and turn on your convection fan if you have one. Lightly oil a 13- × 9-inch (3 L) baking or roasting pan.

Begin with the sauce. Melt the butter in a large pot over medium-high heat. Toss in the onion and garlic; sauté until the textures soften and the flavors brighten, a few minutes. Add all but ½ cup (125 mL) of the milk and bring to a simmer. Whisk in the Dijon, Worcestershire, bay leaves, nutmeg, salt, and pepper. Sprinkle the cornstarch into the remaining ½ cup (125 mL) milk, stirring until smooth. Pour the cornstarch milk into the sauce, stirring until thickened, just a few minutes more. Add the ricotta and Parmesan, stirring until smooth. Stir in as much of the spinach as will fit and continue cooking and stirring as it wilts. Repeat with any remaining spinach.

Assemble the lasagna. Start with a layer of sauce, follow with an even layer of noodles (breaking some up to fill gaps if needed), then alternate all the way to the top, finishing with a layer of sauce. Top with the remaining Parmesan and mozzarella.

Place one long sheet of foil over another the same length. Fold over one long side by ½ inch (1 cm) and crimp tightly; fold and crimp another ½ inch. Open up the two sheets into one larger one and tightly crease the center seam. Lightly oil one side and invert over the pan, covering it fully and crimping the edges tightly. This craftsmanship will help preserve vital moisture in the lasagna. Bake until all the layers have heated through and the noodles have tenderized, about 45 minutes. Remove the foil and bake for another 15 minutes, allowing the cheese topping to lightly brown. Let rest for a few minutes before slicing. Serve and share!

For the sauce
¼ cup (60 mL) of butter (non-dairy if need be)

1 onion, minced

4 garlic cloves, sliced

4 cups (1 L) of dairy, soy, or rice milk

2 tablespoons (30 mL) of Dijon mustard

1 tablespoon (15 mL) of Worcestershire sauce (or tamari for a gluten-free option)

2 bay leaves

1 teaspoon (5 mL) of nutmeg (½ whole nutmeg)

1 teaspoon (5 mL) of salt

1 teaspoon (5 mL) or so of freshly ground pepper

¼ cup (60 mL) of cornstarch

2 cups (500 mL) of ricotta cheese (non-dairy if needed)

2 cups (500 mL) of grated Parmesan cheese (non-dairy if needed)

1 pound (450 g) of fresh baby spinach

For assembly
1½ pounds (675 g) of no-boil lasagna noodles (gluten-free if need be)

1 cup (250 mL) of grated Parmesan cheese (non-dairy if needed)

1 cup (250 mL) of shredded mozzarella cheese (non-dairy if needed)

------------------------------ **TWIST** ------------------------------

Often our reasons for freestyling ideas into dinner have nothing to do with creative indulgence but instead are driven by necessity. This lasagna can be crafted with gluten-free noodles, non-dairy and non-soy milk and cheeses, cornstarch instead of eggs, and tamari instead of Worcestershire.

HOT-AND-SOUR BROTH WITH ASIAN NOODLES

This deliciously addictive soup shows how tasty a dish can be when you balance spiciness with sourness. Its big, bright flavors are simple to stir together, but get ready for a table full of noodle slurpers! SERVES 2 TO 4

8 ounces (225 g) of shiitake mushrooms, thinly sliced

1 carrot, grated

1 cup (250 mL) of frozen shelled edamame

4 cups (1 L) of rich chicken broth

2 tablespoons (30 mL) of soy sauce

1 teaspoon (5 mL) of sambal oelek or your favorite chili-garlic sauce

2 tablespoons (30 mL) of cornstarch

2 tablespoons (30 mL) of rice vinegar

12 ounces (340 g) of udon noodles

2-inch (5 cm) piece of frozen ginger, grated

4 green onions, thinly sliced

1 teaspoon (5 mL) of toasted sesame oil

In your favorite large saucepan, combine the mushrooms, carrot, edamame, chicken broth, soy sauce, and sambal. Bring the works to a simmer over medium-high heat.

Meanwhile, whisk together the cornstarch and rice vinegar in a small bowl. When the soup is simmering, gently stir in the cornstarch mixture; continue to simmer, stirring, until it thickens the soup, just a minute or two.

Stir in the udon noodles and continue cooking and stirring until they're soft and tender, just a few minutes longer. To finish the soup, stir in the grated ginger, green onions, and sesame oil. Serve and share!

> **TWIST**
>
> Hot-and-sour soups are common throughout Southeast Asian cooking, but they don't normally include noodles. This recipe does because I like noodles, and part of freestyling is not feeling constrained by the need to be authentic. Instead, you can draw inspiration from all over the world, stir in your ideas, and just make dinner. It's your kitchen!

BACON MAC 'N' CHEESE

This is perhaps the single tastiest recipe I have ever created. It's an excellent example of how mastery of a basic dish like standard mac and cheese can lead to creative freedom and delicious results. Why not stir bacon into mac and cheese? Why not stir your ideas into more of your cooking? SERVES 4 TO 6, WITH LEFTOVERS

Position a rack toward the bottom of your oven so the mac and cheese can bake evenly in the middle. Preheat the oven to 400°F (200°C) and turn on your convection fan if you have one. Lightly oil your favorite large baking dish.

Fill your largest pot with lots of hot water and lots of salt and put it over lots of heat. Bring the works to a boil and cook the noodles. Review the pasta insights on pages 144 and 147.

While you wait, ready the bread crumb topping. Fill your food processor with the bread and your choice of herb. Pulse until coarse, even crumbs are formed, just a few seconds. With the food processor running, splash in the olive oil, processing just long enough to evenly combine the works. Don't grind the crumbs too finely—the coarser the crumbs, the crispier they'll be once baked.

Begin the sauce by putting the bacon in a large saucepan over medium-high heat. Splash in enough water to just barely cover it. Stir frequently with a wooden spoon. As the water simmers, the bacon will begin to cook. Then, as the water evaporates, the bacon will render, releasing its fat. Lastly, it will crisp as the flavorful bacon fat heats past the boiling point of water into the flavor zone. Adjust the heat as needed, keeping the bacon sizzling but not smoking and burning. Stir and be patient, until the bacon is evenly cooked and crisp. Using a slotted spoon, transfer the bacon bits to paper towels, leaving the fat behind for building the sauce.

Continued

For the bread crumb topping
½ loaf of Italian bread, torn or cut into chunks

1 tablespoon (15 mL) of your favorite dried herb, such as oregano, thyme, sage, or rosemary

A few good splashes of extra-virgin olive oil

For the mac and cheese
1 pound (450 g) of penne

12 slices of bacon, chopped

2 onions, diced

4 garlic cloves, minced

⅔ cup (150 mL) of all-purpose flour

4 cups (1 L) of any milk

1 cup (250 mL) of whipping cream

2 tablespoons (30 mL) of Dijon mustard

1 tablespoon (15 mL) of paprika

1 or 2 teaspoons (5 or 10 mL) of hot sauce

1 teaspoon (5 mL) of salt

1 pound (450 g) of your favorite aged Cheddar cheese, shredded

Add the onions and garlic to the hot bacon fat; sauté as the textures soften and flavors brighten, 5 minutes or so. Evenly sprinkle the flour over the onions, then stir it in well. The bacon fat will absorb the flour and create a thick paste. Continue cooking, getting rid of the raw flour taste, just a minute or two. Whisking constantly, pour in the milk and cream, then gently stir as the sauce thickens, about 10 minutes.

When the noodles are al dente, drain them and return them to the pot. To finish the sauce, smoothly stir in the mustard, paprika, hot sauce, and salt, then mix in the cheese and the bacon bits. Pour the sauce over the hot, steamy noodles and stir the works together.

Pour the creamy mac and cheese into the prepared baking dish. Sprinkle evenly with the seasoned bread crumbs. Transfer to the oven, lower the temperature to 350°F (180°C), and bake until lightly golden brown and bubbly, 30 minutes or so. Serve and share!

TWIST

Feel free to stir a wide variety of other tasty treats into your mac and cheese. I enjoy a store-bought rotisserie chicken shredded into the works. Broccoli, peas, chickpeas, and other vegetables can all make an appearance. Salmon, scallops, and lobster can star too!

WHOLE WHEAT SPAETZLE WITH BABY SPINACH

Usually noodles are manufactured by a giant faraway machine. For this dish you get to make them yourself. Get some water simmering, quickly stir together a rustic, hearty batter, and be boiling noodles in no time! Best of all, you can toss in a huge dose of bright green spinach and fill your table with homemade healthy flavors. SERVES 2 TO 4

For the spaetzle batter, in a medium bowl, whisk together the flour, cornstarch, nutmeg, salt, and pepper, evenly distributing the finer powders amidst the coarser ones. In another bowl, whisk together the eggs and milk. Stir the wet ingredients into the dry ingredients, forming a firm, sticky batter.

Meanwhile, fill your largest pot with lots of hot water and lots of salt and put it over lots of heat. Bring to a boil. Position a colander with ¼-inch (5 mm) holes over the simmering water. Melt the finishing butter in your largest skillet over medium-high heat.

Transfer some or all of the relaxed batter to the colander and use a rubber spatula to force it through the holes into the simmering water below. (If you don't have a colander try a standard box grater held on its side. Load it with batter and rub the works back and forth over and through its largest holes.) The spaetzle cook very quickly. They'll sink, then almost immediately float to the surface when they're done. Stir gently so they don't stick together. Strain them out with a slotted spoon and spill them into the melted butter, tossing gently and coating evenly. Repeat with any remaining batter. If you like, continue sautéing until the noodles crisp a bit.

Drain all but ¼ cup (60 mL) or so of the starchy spaetzle cooking water. Cram all the spinach into the pot, cover, and place over medium-high heat. After a minute or two, stir the spinach until it is all wilted. Stir in the spaetzle. Serve and share!

For the spaetzle batter
1 cup (250 mL) of whole wheat or all-purpose flour
1 tablespoon (15 mL) of cornstarch
1 teaspoon (5 mL) of freshly grated nutmeg
¼ teaspoon (1 mL) of salt
Lots of freshly ground pepper
2 eggs
½ cup (125 mL) of milk

For finishing the spaetzle
¼ cup (60 mL) of butter
10 ounces (280 g) of fresh baby spinach

TWIST

Feel free to experiment with the flour in the batter. As you cross the spectrum from 100% whole wheat through 50/50 to 100% white flour, you'll taste the difference in the dumplings. Whole wheat produces a coarser, heartier, softer noodle, whereas all-purpose flour yields a chewier, firmer noodle.

GOAT CHEESE GNOCCHI WITH SAGE BUTTERNUT SQUASH SAUCE

Gnocchi are thick, soft dumplings that can be based on several ingredients, including wheat, potatoes, bread crumbs, or a mixture of flour, eggs, and cheese as in this recipe. SERVES 4

For the butternut squash sauce

¼ cup (60 mL) of butter

2 onions, minced

4 garlic cloves, minced

1 medium butternut squash, peeled, seeded, and cut in ½-inch (1 cm) cubes

1 cup (250 mL) of water

½ teaspoon (2 mL) of salt

Lots of freshly ground pepper

Leaves from 1 bunch of fresh sage, thinly sliced (or 1 tablespoon/ 15 mL dried sage)

For the gnocchi

A 10-ounce (280 g) log of soft goat cheese

2 eggs

¼ cup (60 mL) of grated Parmigiano-Reggiano cheese

1 tablespoon (15 mL) of butter, melted

1 teaspoon (5 mL) of salt

3/4 cup (175 mL) of all-purpose flour

Begin with the sauce. In your favorite sauté pan, melt the butter over medium-high heat. Add the onions and garlic; sauté as the textures soften and the flavors brighten, 5 minutes or so. Toss in the butternut squash, water, salt, and pepper. Gently stir together, combining the flavors. Reduce the heat to a slow, steady simmer, cover tightly, and continue cooking, stirring occasionally, until the squash is soft and delicious, another 15 minutes or so. Stir the sauce to break up the squash further, but don't turn it into a paste.

Meanwhile, start the gnocchi. In your stand mixer or food processor, beat or process the goat cheese and eggs until smooth. Add the Parmesan cheese, butter, and salt. Continue mixing until light and fluffy. If using a food processor, transfer the mixture to a bowl. Gently stir in the flour with a wooden spoon until a smooth dough forms.

Cut the dough in half. Lightly flour your hands, the work surface, and the dough. Roll each piece of dough out into a long, even rope about ½ inch (1 cm) thick. Cut crosswise into 1-inch (2.5 cm) pieces.

Bring a large pot of salted water to a boil. Add half the gnocchi (to avoid crowding the pot). Cook until the water returns to a boil and the tender gnocchi rise to the top, 3 or 4 minutes. Using a slotted spoon, transfer the gnocchi to the sauce. Repeat with the remaining gnocchi.

Stir the sage into the sauce; continue cooking until everything is heated through and aromatic, just a few minutes more. Serve and share!

- - - - - - - - - - - **TWIST** - - - - - - - - - - -

Any aromatic fresh green herb will work in this dish. Try tarragon, oregano, basil, chives, green onions, rosemary, savory, thyme, or even mint. Great big heaping spoonfuls of an old-fashioned homemade basil pesto are delicious too.

HANDMADE

VEGETABLES SIDES and VEGETARIAN

VEGETABLES, SIDES & VEGETARIAN

FRESH CHILI

A hearty batch of spicy chili is one of the world's great comfort foods, but it often takes hours of simmering to get there. The solution? Leave out the meat! You can drop the long cooking time and pick up a much brighter-flavored chili instead. **SERVES 4**

1 tablespoon (15 mL) of
    vegetable oil

1 onion, sliced

4 garlic cloves, sliced

1 teaspoon (5 mL) of cumin seeds

3 bell peppers, your favorite
    colors, diced

1 jalapeño, Cubanelle, or poblano
    pepper, seeded and diced

A 19-ounce (540 mL) can of black
    or red kidney beans, drained
    and rinsed

1 cup (250 mL) of frozen corn

1 cup (250 mL) of tomato juice or water

The zest and juice of 1 lime

½ teaspoon (2 mL) of salt

1 bunch of fresh cilantro, chopped

Splash the oil into your favorite large, heavy skillet or saucepan over medium-high heat. Toss in the onion, garlic, and cumin seeds; sauté until the textures soften and the flavors brighten, just 2 or 3 minutes. Add the bell peppers and chili pepper to the mix and continue sautéing while they too soften and brighten.

Add the beans, corn, tomato juice, lime zest and juice, and salt. Bring to a simmer, thoroughly heating everything through. Serve and share with handfuls of cilantro sprinkled about!

----------------------- TWIST -----------------------
You won't miss the meat in this chili because it includes both a grain—corn—and a legume—the beans—the two essential ingredients that allow your body to create vegetarian protein.

LENTIL CHIA BURGERS

This is the holy grail of vegetarian cooking: a hearty, tasty burger that's so firm and meaty that no one misses its beefy origins. The secret? Lots of healthy ingredients—and chia seeds. These magical seeds are not only good for you but also good for the burger. Absent the binding properties of ground meat, they help the works hold together firmly. **MAKES 10 BURGERS OR SO, ENOUGH TO FREEZE A FEW FOR ANOTHER TIME**

Cook the lentils first. Bring the lentils, water, and salt to a simmer in a medium saucepan, cover tightly, and continue simmering until they are soft and tender, 15 to 20 minutes. Drain off any excess water. Measure 2 cups (500 mL) of the lentils and enjoy the left-overs as a snack!

Meanwhile, for the burgers, splash the oil into your favorite large, heavy skillet over medium-high heat. Toss in the onion, garlic, and mushrooms; sauté as the textures soften and the flavors brighten. The mixture will go through several stages from dry to wet and back to dry. The secret is to continue cooking until the moisture that's released evaporates. This will help the burgers hold together.

Scrape the mushroom mixture into your food processor. Add the bread crumbs, nut butter, chia seeds, miso, soy sauce, and thyme. Pulse until smooth. Transfer to a bowl and mix in the lentils. Then stir in the sweet potato, which will preserve the texture and appearance of this brightly flavored nutritional powerhouse.

Let the burger mixture rest for about 15 minutes, until the amazing properties of the magical water-loving chia seeds kick in, absorbing the surrounding moisture, gelling, and firming the mixture. Using your hands, gently and firmly form about 10 evenly shaped patties. You're ready to cook! (You can freeze unused burgers for another day. Wrap individual burgers in plastic wrap, then freeze in large freezer bags for a month or two. When that day comes, thaw them before cooking. They'll be just as delicious.)

Pan-fry, grill, barbecue, or bake in a 400°F (200°C) oven until browned, and heated through, 15 minutes or so. Build a burger your way with a great bun and your favorite toppings. Serve and share!

For the lentils
1 cup (250 mL) of green lentils

3 cups (750 mL) of water

½ teaspoon (2 mL) of salt

For the burgers
2 tablespoons (30 mL) of vegetable oil

1 onion, chopped

4 garlic cloves, chopped

8 ounces (225 g) of mushrooms, sliced

1 cup (250 mL) of dry bread crumbs

½ cup (125 mL) of peanut, almond, or other nut butter

¼ cup (60 mL) of chia seeds

2 tablespoons (30 mL) of any miso paste

2 tablespoons (30 mL) of soy sauce

2 tablespoons (30 mL) of dried thyme

2 cups (500 mL) of grated unpeeled sweet potato (about 1 medium potato)

Rolls or buns

Your favorite toppings and condiments

- - - - - - - TWIST - - - - - - -

Experiment with the seasonings in this burger. You can easily substitute other herbs for the thyme—rosemary, oregano, or sage work well. You can also add a southwestern theme with chili powder and cumin.

PAN-ROASTED ZUCCHINI & CHERRY TOMATOES

This simple combination of vegetables and flavors has iconic status at my family's table. It's my go-to dish when I have a few zucchini kicking around. They're the perfect vegetable for this high-heat method, browning and flavoring easily as you sauté them. SERVES 4

2 zucchini (8 inches/20 cm or so each), cubed

1 large onion, diced

1 tablespoon (15 mL) of vegetable oil

¼ teaspoon (1 mL) of salt

Lots of freshly ground pepper

1 pint (500 mL) of cherry tomatoes, halved

1 teaspoon (5 mL) of dried oregano

Heat your favorite large, heavy skillet or sauté pan over medium-high heat. Toss the zucchini and onion into a large bowl. Splash in the oil, and sprinkle with the salt and pepper. Toss the works together.

Transfer the zucchini and onions to the hot pan. Sauté and sizzle, browning lightly as the textures soften and the flavors brighten, 5 minutes or so. Add the tomatoes and oregano. Stir and cook the works until they're thoroughly heated through and smell delicious, just a minute or two. Serve and share!

TWIST

Once you know the basics you can twist them, but the best way to small-dice an onion will never change:

- Trim the root and stalk ends off the onion.

- Cut the onion in half lengthwise.

- Peel off the remaining skin layers from each half.

- Lay the peeled onion halves flat on their cut sides.

- Slice as thinly as you can, first in one direction, then the other. You don't need to make any horizontal cuts—parallel to the cutting board—they're awkward and unnecessary. The onion's own natural layers do that job for you. They'll naturally separate into smaller pieces.

SECRET NUTMEG SPINACH

Maybe—just maybe—you can distract the kids from the fact that they're eating spinach by getting them to guess the mysterious spice in the works. Remind them that it flavors kid-friendly hot dogs, ketchup, and doughnuts. It might just work! SERVES 4 TO 6

Melt the butter in a large saucepan over medium heat. If you like, continue cooking the butter until it is brown and smells nutty. Either way, add the onion and sprinkle in the nutmeg, salt, and pepper. Cook until the onion is light golden brown and softened, just a few minutes.

Pile in the spinach and gently stir the works together, evenly distributing all the flavors. Keep an eye on things. The dish is done and at its best as soon as the spinach heats through, wilts down a bit, brightens and lightens, just a few minutes more. If you cook it too long, it will darken, release all its moisture, and get soupy-dreary, so serve and share now!

2 tablespoons (30 mL) of butter

1 onion, chopped

1 whole nutmeg, grated (about 2 teaspoons/10 mL)

¼ teaspoon (1 mL) of salt

Lots of freshly ground pepper

16 ounces (450 g) of fresh baby spinach

TWIST

There are many ways to stir *your* twists into *your* cooking. One of my favorites is browning butter every chance I get. The flavor dividends are more than worth the time and patient vigilance invested. When you brown butter, you caramelize various natural sugars within it, thus unlocking a much deeper, caramelized, even nutty flavor. Frankly, it's addictive.

Simply melt the butter and keep on cooking. Swirl gently, and eventually the moisture in the butter will heat, steam, foam, and evaporate away. Once that moisture is gone, the butter fat left behind can then rise in temperature—past the boiling point of water—into the browning, flavoring zone. Take it as far as you dare—the deeper the color, the deeper the flavor. Just be ready! Turning off the heat doesn't stop the cooking and browning. The line between brown and burnt black is quickly crossed, so you'll need to add something to the butter to cool it down—in this case, onions.

AROMATIC STEAMED BROCCOLI

A bunch of broccoli is one of the easiest ways to get a pile of dark green, healthy flavor on your table. But don't toss the tougher stems. Just slice them thinly and give them a head start. **SERVES 4**

1 large bunch of broccoli

1 tablespoon (15 mL) of extra-virgin olive oil

1 onion, minced

2 garlic cloves, sliced

1 or 2 bay leaves

½ teaspoon (2 mL) of salt

Lots of freshly ground pepper

Cut the broccoli into small florets. Thinly slice the thick stalks, discarding the tough ends. Splash about ½ inch (1 cm) water into your favorite large saucepan. Splash in the oil, then toss in the sliced broccoli stems along with the onion, garlic, bay leaves, salt, and pepper. Cover and bring the works to a simmer over medium-high heat. Cook until the stems soften, 3 or 4 minutes.

Toss in the broccoli florets, cover tightly, lower the heat, and steam the broccoli until it is tender, aromatic, and bright green, 5 minutes or so. The water will evaporate just as the broccoli finishes cooking. Serve and share!

TWIST

Steaming is an excellent way to cook broccoli. The moist heat is fast and efficient and doesn't drain away flavor—and thus nutrients—the way submerging in boiling water does. Depending on your table's preferences, feel free to skip the onions, garlic, and bay leaves, or to add even more aromatic character with other herbs such as thyme or tarragon. Curry powder is an excellent addition as well.

SPICY ASIAN GREENS

You can find many mainstream Asian greens at your supermarket these days. They're among the healthiest and tastiest vegetable options you have and are super easy to cook and add flavor to. SERVES 2 TO 4

Remove and discard the tough stalks from the mushrooms. Thinly slice the mushrooms or simply cut or tear them into quarters. Starting at the leaf end, cut the bok choy into 2-inch (5 cm) pieces, discarding the tough base. Place the leaves in a strainer or colander and rinse well, removing any sand that sometimes clings to this tasty veggie. It's OK for water to stick to the leaves—the moisture will help them cook.

Splash the vegetable and sesame oils into your favorite large saucepan over medium-high heat, then toss in the mushrooms. Sauté until their textures soften and the flavors brighten, 2 or 3 minutes. Stir in the soy sauce, sambal, and ginger. Top with the wet greens. Continue cooking and stirring until the greens wilt, brighten, tenderize, and absorb the aromatic flavors, no more than 3 or 4 minutes. Serve and share!

8 ounces (225 g) of shiitake mushrooms

1 large or 6 baby bok choy

1 teaspoon (5 mL) of any vegetable oil

1 teaspoon (5 mL) of toasted sesame oil

2 tablespoons (30 mL) of soy sauce

4 teaspoons (20 mL) of sambal oelek or your favorite chili-garlic sauce

¼ cup (60 mL) of grated frozen ginger

TWIST

This basic aromatic steaming method works for any exotic green at your supermarket: bok choy, pak choi, choy sum, napa cabbage, Chinese cabbage, broccoli rabe, or basic baby spinach.

PROSCIUTTO ROAST ASPARAGUS

Dress up simple asparagus with slices of prosciutto. This is the sort of spectacular dish that looks a lot harder than it really is and automatically makes any meat or fish next to it look better. **SERVES 6 TO 8**

6 to 8 slices of thinly sliced prosciutto

2 bunches of fresh asparagus, thick or thin, tougher ends trimmed

2 tablespoons (30 mL) of extra-virgin olive oil

Lots of freshly ground pepper

Preheat your oven to 500°F (260°C) and turn on your convection fan if you have one.

Lay a slice of prosciutto on your work surface stretching away from you. Gather up a pile of asparagus spears, 5 or 6 larger ones or 10 thinner ones. Roll them tightly in the prosciutto. Arrange seam side down on a small baking sheet. Repeat with the remaining asparagus and prosciutto. Brush each roll all over with a bit of olive oil. Sprinkle with pepper (the salty prosciutto will season as well). Bake until the prosciutto crisps a bit and the asparagus brightens and tenderizes, about 10 minutes. Serve and share!

---- **TWIST** ----

Spread a bit of your favorite mustard or other condiment on the inside of the prosciutto before you top it with the asparagus. Tapenade, pesto, and dried tomato paste are all fair game too.

GRILLED EGGPLANT

Eggplant is often overlooked in the kitchen, but once you've mastered the simple art of grilling it and discovered its incredible creamy texture and delicious sweetness, you'll never forget this luxurious vegetable again. Especially if you jazz it up with lots of Mediterranean flavors!

SERVES 4, OR 6 IF 6 CAN SHARE

Build a hardwood fire and let it die down to a thick bed of hot glowing coals, or prepare and preheat your barbecue or grill to its highest setting.

Trim the blossom end off of the eggplants and cut them in half lengthwise. Brush the cut sides with olive oil and lightly sprinkle with salt and pepper. Position cut side down on the grill and begin cooking. Take a peek occasionally. The flesh will soften as it cooks, changing from opaque to translucent. After 15 minutes or so, when the flesh is translucent and soft, it's at its best—time to flip it over.

Evenly spread the tapenade over the grilled cut side of each eggplant, then sprinkle with the feta. Continue grilling as the skin side softens, the toppings warm through, and the eggplant finishes cooking, 2 or 3 minutes longer. Serve and share!

2 large eggplants

½ cup (125 mL) of extra-virgin olive oil

½ teaspoon (2 mL) of salt

Lots of freshly ground pepper

¼ cup (60 mL) of black olive tapenade

8 ounces (225 g) of feta cheese, crumbled

TWIST

Instead of using tapenade, you can easily just chop up a handful of pitted black olives. Pesto or dried tomato paste also works well. Boursin-style cream cheese is delicious.

BACON CARAWAY CABBAGE

Sometimes it feels like cheating when you add bacon to vegetables, but not when cabbage is on the menu. This hearty vegetable seems custom designed to soak up the flavors of crispy bacon. And besides, when was the last time you thought of cabbage as a treat? SERVES 4

8 slices of bacon, chopped

2 tablespoons (30 mL) of caraway seeds

1 green cabbage

¼ cup (60 mL) of cider vinegar

¼ cup (60 mL) of water

Begin the sauce by tossing the bacon into a large saucepan over medium-high heat, then splash in enough water to just barely cover it. Stir frequently with a wooden spoon. As the water simmers, the bacon will begin to cook. Then, as the water evaporates, the bacon will render, releasing its fat. Lastly, it will crisp as the flavorful bacon fat heats past the boiling point of water into the flavor zone. Adjust the heat as needed, keeping the bacon sizzling but not smoking and burning. Stir and be patient, until the bacon is fully and evenly cooked and crisp. Stir in the caraway seeds and sauté briefly, brightening the flavors and cooling the bacon enough to keep it from burning.

Meanwhile, cut the cabbage in half lengthwise and cut out and discard the tough, woody core. Slice the cabbage into thin ribbons.

When the bacon and caraway seeds are ready, pour in the vinegar and water. Top the works with the cabbage. Cook, cramming and stirring as the cabbage wilts, 5 minutes or so. Serve and share!

TWIST

I prefer cider vinegar with cabbage, but really any vinegar will do. Instead of caraway seeds, try cumin or fennel seeds. You can even skip the seeds and stir some curry powder or mustard into the works.

HOUSE MASHED POTATOES

Of all the recipes in this book, this one is perhaps the most essential. I mean, imagine life without mashed potatoes. Better yet, imagine all the different ways you can transform a batch of simple spuds into a signature masterpiece. SERVES 4

Cut the potatoes into large chunks and steam or boil them until they're tender, about 20 minutes.

Meanwhile, gently heat 1 cup (250 mL) of any one of the following: milk, cream, butter, or chicken broth.

Consider your many finishing choices and choose ½ cup (125 mL) of one of the following:

FOR LIGHTER, CREAMIER TEXTURE AND FLAVOR: mascarpone cheese, cream cheese, sour cream, yogurt, Boursin cheese

FOR STRONGER, ASSERTIVE CHEESY FLAVOR: Cheddar cheese, blue cheese, Parmesan cheese, smoked Gouda cheese

FOR DISTINCTIVE AROMATIC CHARACTER: fresh basil pesto, olive tapenade, barbecue sauce

Drain the spuds and return them to the pot or transfer them to a large bowl. Add the warmed liquid and your flavoring choice to the hot, steamy potatoes. Season with salt and pepper. Mash away until your potatoes are as country-rustic or city-smooth as you like.

If you like, stir in a finishing flavor or two:

- lots and lots of your favorite chopped herb
- a few chopped green onions or a handful of chopped chives
- a few slices of crispy, crunchy bacon and as much or as little of the rendered fat as you like
- anything else you can think of!

Make up a name for your masterpiece, then serve and share!

2 pounds (900 g) of your favorite potatoes (unpeeled)

> **TWIST**
>
> Mashed potatoes are a blank canvas just waiting for you to stir in your ideas. There are many great suggestions here, but don't feel limited by them. Over the years I've stirred every cheese on the planet into my spud bowl. I've even reduced a full bottle of red wine to a syrup and stirred it in with cream to create shocking pink potatoes. The sky really is the limit.

SPICED FRENCH FRIES

It's fun gearing up for a good old-fashioned french fry. Creating a basket of crisp and golden fries is a noble quest well worthy of your passion. The secret is the same as it's ever been: a two-step frying. And don't stop there. Try tossing in a bit of spice too! SERVES 4 TO 6

For the spiced french fries

3 or 4 large russet potatoes (unpeeled)

2 quarts (2 L) of vegetable or peanut oil

1 teaspoon (5 mL) of curry powder, chili powder, or your favorite spice

1 teaspoon (5 mL) of salt

For the spicy ketchup dip

¼ cup (60 mL) of ketchup

¼ cup (60 mL) of mayonnaise

1 teaspoon (5 mL) of curry powder, chili powder, or your favorite spice

TWIST

Feel free to be wildly experimental with the spice flavors on the fries and in the dipping sauce—they're not the sort of thing to take too seriously. Better to let loose and clean out the fridge a bit! And don't forget the classics either. As tasty as curry-spiced fries are, nothing beats tossing crisp golden fries with gold-standard sea salt and lots of freshly ground pepper.

Prep the potatoes first. Wash the spuds under lots of running water. Carefully cut them into evenly shaped french fries—large or small, doesn't matter, as long as they're even—placing the strips in a large bowl of cold water as you go.

Ready the frying oil for the first cook, the blanching. Pour the oil into your largest, deepest pot, filling no more than the halfway point. Heat the oil until a deep-fat thermometer reads 250°F (120°C).

Drain the potatoes and dry them well on paper towels or a kitchen cloth. Working in batches if necessary, carefully transfer them to the hot oil. Gently stir as they bubble away, cooking, heating, and softening, about 5 minutes. The oil's temperature is not high enough to brown them but it is high enough to improve their texture and ready them for the much higher temperatures ahead. Strain them out and drain them on paper towels. (This step can be done several hours ahead.)

While the potatoes drain, make the spicy ketchup dip. In a small bowl, stir together the ketchup, mayonnaise, and curry powder. Set aside.

Heat the oil to 375°F (190°C). Return the potatoes to the oil and commence frying. Figure on 15, even 20 minutes. The much higher temperature will caramelize the various sugars within the potatoes, transforming them into golden-brown and crispy—yet inside simultaneously smooth and creamy—french fries. Strain the magnificent fries out with a handheld strainer and drain on paper towels. Transfer to a large paper bag, add the curry powder and salt, and gently toss until the flavors are evenly distributed. Serve and share with the dip!

CRACKED POTATOES

Bake a few potatoes till tender, smash 'em down and bake 'em again, then top 'em with your favorite cheese. Intensely delicious and irrevocably memorable. One of my all-time best side dishes. Just saying . . . **SERVES 4**

Preheat your oven to 400°F (200°C) and turn on your convection fan if you have one. Bake the potatoes directly on the middle rack until tender, 45 minutes or so. Remove the potatoes and crank the oven to 450°F (230°C).

Lightly oil a baking pan or cookie sheet. With a small plate, gently push down on each potato, flattening it and spreading it out to twice its original size. Arrange the potatoes in the baking pan. Evenly drizzle each potato with an overflowing tablespoon of olive oil. Season with salt and pepper.

Bake the cracked potatoes until they're golden brown and crispy, 40 minutes or so. Devour as is or evenly top each potato with cheese and return to the oven until the cheese is bubbly and gooey, another few minutes. Serve and share!

4 baking potatoes

¼ cup (60 mL) of extra-virgin olive oil

A sprinkle or two of salt

Lots of freshly ground pepper

1 cup (250 mL) of your favorite shredded cheese

------- TWIST -------

Try sprinkling a bit of spice into the flavor works. Try whole spice seeds—fennel, coriander, cumin, or caraway. And I'm sure if you put your mind to it, you can figure out a way to sneak a few slices of bacon into the works!

BREAKFAST SPUDS

What a great way to start your day—especially if you bake the spuds the night before. Then it's straight to flavor in the a.m. The ingredients in this recipe are always comfortable together, but this time it's the awakening aroma of the bacon-in-the-pan-first that gives this dish such exalted status. SERVES 4 TO 6

24 baby potatoes

8 slices of thick-cut bacon, diced

2 onions, sliced

1 cup (250 mL) or so of shredded Cheddar cheese

1 bunch of fresh chives, sliced

The day before, bake the potatoes in a baking pan at 400°F (200°C) until tender, 30 minutes or so. Let cool, then refrigerate for the morning and enjoy your evening.

Match your favorite large skillet with the sun, medium-high heat, and a lid for later. Toss in the bacon, then splash in enough water to just barely cover it. Stir frequently with a wooden spoon. As the water simmers, the bacon will begin to cook. Then, as the water evaporates, the bacon will render, releasing its fat. Lastly, it will crisp as the flavorful bacon fat heats past the boiling point of water into the flavor zone. Adjust the heat as needed, keeping the bacon sizzling but not smoking and burning. Stir and be patient, until the bacon is fully and evenly cooked and crisp. Strain out and reserve the proceeds. Drain off half the fat. Add the onions to the hot fat and sauté until golden brown and softened, a few minutes.

Meanwhile, flatten each of the potatoes with your palm or the bottom of a mug or jar. Firmly nestle them among the aromatic onions, making sure they contact the hot pan. Continue cooking without stirring—just sizzling—until crispy, 5 minutes or so. Stir in the bacon and top with the cheese. Cover with the almost forgotten lid, turn off the heat, and let rest, blending flavors and melting the cheese, 3 or 4 minutes. Sprinkle with the chives, serve, and share!

------------------- TWIST -------------------
A firm mastery of the basics will serve you well as you cook your heart out. Even sound. The sound of sizzle. Listen, and without looking you can reliably tell when a pan's heat is in the bland nothing-happening zone, the browning-crisping-delicious zone (the sound of success!), or horribly possibly the burning, blackening, ruined end of things.

AUTHENTIC RISOTTO

Authenticity is not about perfection. It's not about right or wrong. It's about the quest. Finding the spirit of a dish. The integrity of doing it the way it's always been done with the same things that have always been used. Risotto is a common northern Italian dish of tender, creamy rice. The exact ingredients to craft a nearly identical version are easily found in North American grocery stores. You can reliably produce this deeply satisfying classic and serve as an ambassador of its humble roots at your table. **SERVES 4 TO 6**

In a large pot, bring the chicken broth to a gentle simmer.

Splash the oil into your favorite medium saucepan over medium-high heat. When it's hot, toss in the onion and garlic. Sauté as the textures soften and the flavors brighten, a few minutes. Add the rice and keep on stirring, toasting the grains in the sizzling oil. They'll transform from pure white to almost entirely opaque right in front of you. Their starches are warmed up and ready to dissolve.

Pour in the wine and stir constantly as the rice quickly absorbs the fragrant liquid. Lower the heat, then add the simmering broth, a ladleful at a time, stirring constantly as you go until most of the liquid is absorbed before adding more. The simmering liquid coaxes the starch out of the rice. As that starch emerges, it immediately thickens the broth, adding immeasurably and memorably to its creaminess. In 15 minutes or so, the rice will soften into a delicious al dente delight, each and every grain separate and coated in creamy goodness. Don't let it cook to a mush!

Remove from the heat and stir in the cheese, butter, and herbs. Serve immediately and share your risotto while it's at its authentic best!

8 cups (2 L) or more of good chicken broth

2 tablespoons (30 mL) of extra-virgin olive oil

1 onion, minced

4 garlic cloves, minced

2 cups (500 mL) of arborio rice

1 cup (250 mL) of your favorite Italian white or red wine

1 cup (250 mL) of grated Grana Padano Parmigiano-Reggiano cheese

1 tablespoon (15 mL) or so of butter

Leaves from a few sprigs, even a full bunch, of thyme or any fresh herb, minced

---
TWIST

In Italy there are too many versions of risotto to count, and every single one is authentic, thus your honorable experimentation is welcome into the ongoing annals of this classic dish.

There are many ways to craft a chicken broth. My favorite is to simply simmer the bones and bits from last night's chicken dinner with onions and a bay leaf. An hour or two usually does it. Alternatively, you can hack up a store-bought rotisserie chicken and simmer it for an hour or two.

BACON & BLUE CHEESE RISOTTO

The heart of a true risotto includes room for the cook's improvised flavors. This version is one of my favorite riffs. I mean, even if you have a thing against blue cheese, you'll get over it when you taste bacon with blue cheese. Magic. SERVES 4 TO 6

4 slices of bacon, chopped

1 onion, chopped

4 garlic cloves, chopped

2 cups (500 mL) of arborio rice

1 cup (250 mL) of your favorite
  hearty red wine

8 cups (2 L) of good chicken broth

Leaves from 2 sprigs of fresh
  rosemary, chopped

1 cup (250 mL) of crumbled
  blue cheese, such as Gorgonzola

Review all the risotto insight found in the basic recipe on page 205. This dish is inspired by that one. Get to cooking, and along the way stir in these flavor variations.

BEGIN WITH BACON Crisp the bacon first, reserving the bits and using the tasty sizzling fat to sauté the onion and garlic.

RED WINE A hearty red wine is needed to match the blue cheese. Splash it in when the grains are done toasting.

ROSEMARY Perhaps the heartiest of the fresh herbs. Stir it in when the risotto is creamy but still al dente, thus preserving its intense yet delicate fresh flavor.

BLUE CHEESE Use a good one. Gorgonzola is authentically Italian—you can bet your bacon they stir it into their risotto pot! Add it last and serve straight away.

TWIST

Blue cheese is extreme cheese. Cheddar—especially aged—is a bit more mellow and mainstream. As you experiment with risottos, feel free to range down the cheese spectrum toward classic savory Parmesan. Really, any of your favorite cheeses are fair game. Try Boursin for a real treat.

BARLEY ASPARAGUS RISOTTO

Barley grains easily succumb to the same slow, steady treatment that coaxes greatness out of the arborio rice grains that anchor classic Italian risotto. Barley's distinctive chewy yet tender texture makes this dish addictively delicious. **SERVES 4 TO 6**

Review all the risotto insight found in the basic recipe on page 205. This dish is inspired by that one.

Bring the chicken broth to a gentle simmer. Splash the oil into a medium saucepan over medium-high heat. Add the onions and garlic; sauté as the textures soften and the flavors brighten, 3 or 4 minutes. Stir the barley into the works, coating each grain with a thin film of oil.

Pour in the wine and stir for a few moments as it's quickly absorbed. Lower the heat and begin adding the simmering broth, a ladleful at a time, stirring constantly as you go, allowing the liquid to be absorbed before adding more. Continue until you've crafted a tender, creamy risotto, 45 minutes or so.

Stir in the asparagus and continue cooking just long enough for its colors to brighten and its texture to soften, 3 or 4 minutes. Remove from the heat, season the works with salt and pepper, and stir in the savory cheese.

8 cups (2 L) of good chicken broth

2 tablespoons (30 mL) of vegetable oil

2 onions, chopped

4 garlic cloves, minced

1 cup (250 mL) of pearl barley

½ cup (125 mL) of your favorite white wine

1 bunch of fresh asparagus, trimmed, cut in 1-inch (2.5 cm) pieces

1 teaspoon (5 mL) of salt

Lots of freshly ground pepper

1 cup (250 mL) of grated Parmigiano-Reggiano cheese

TWIST

Beyond asparagus, many green vegetables add flavor and flair to a batch of any risotto. Try handfuls of baby spinach, small broccoli florets, or a few handfuls of frozen peas or edamame beans.

CANADIAN GRAIN PILAF

Grains made Canada great—we grow the best in the world. Not only is this dish wildly healthy, memorably hearty, and addictively delicious, but it's also an homage to the patchwork quilt of farms on the Great Plains. The rice substitute Rice of the Prairies is a variety of oat. Look for the Cavena Nuda brand at the Bulk Barn or mysmartfoods.com. **EASILY SERVES 4 TO 6, WITH LOTS OF TASTY LEFTOVERS**

½ cup (125 mL) of wheat berries
(whole wheat grains)

½ cup (125 mL) of barley

½ cup (125 mL) of wild rice

½ cup (125 mL) of steel-cut
rolled oats

½ cup (125 mL) of Rice of
the Prairies

½ cup (125 mL) of frozen corn

6 cups (1.5 L) of chicken broth
or water

1 teaspoon (5 mL) of salt

1 bay leaf

Preheat your oven to 325°F (160°C) and turn on your convection fan if you have one.

In your favorite large ovenproof pot, combine the wheat berries, barley, wild rice, oats, Rice of the Prairies, corn, broth, salt, and bay leaf. Bring to a simmer over medium-high heat. Cover tightly and bake until the grains tenderize and absorb all the surrounding liquid, 60 minutes or so. Serve and share!

TWIST

Feel free to stir in a few handfuls of finishing fresh herb flavor. Thyme, tarragon, rosemary, and sage are all excellent.

It's just as easy to make a lot as a little, and once you taste these grains you'll be happy to have leftovers. In the coming days, toss them into any soup, stew, or green salad. They're especially good tossed with a bit of sharp dressing and served as is. You can easily freeze them for future projects as well.

CURRY ROAST CAULIFLOWER & CHICKPEAS

Ordinarily, cooked cauliflower is about as exciting as eating steamed white rice on the corner of Plain and Bland. But toss in lots of fragrant spices and a good golden-brown roasting, and enjoy the parade of colorful flavors that goes marching by! SERVES 4 TO 6

Preheat your oven to 375°F (190°C) and turn on your convection fan if you have one.

In a large bowl, toss together the cauliflower, onions, garlic, chickpeas, oil, curry powder, cumin seeds, fennel seeds, coriander seeds, and salt, evenly distributing the vegetables and spice flavors. Pour the works into a 13- × 9-inch (3 L) baking pan. Roast, stirring once or twice, until golden brown, about an hour. Serve and share!

1 cauliflower, cut in small florets

2 onions, diced

Cloves from 1 head of garlic, halved

A 19-ounce (540 mL) can of chickpeas, drained and rinsed

¼ cup (60 mL) of any vegetable oil or melted butter

1 heaping tablespoon (18 mL) of your favorite curry powder

1 tablespoon (15 mL) or so of cumin seeds

1 tablespoon (15 mL) or so of fennel seeds

1 tablespoon (15 mL) of coriander seeds

½ teaspoon (2 mL) of salt

---------------------- TWIST ----------------------

There are many ways you can tweak the flavors in this dish. Perhaps the most important, though, doesn't involve the ingredients, it's about the method itself—the potential flavors of roasting. There's a big difference between a pan with a bit of color here and there and a pan full of fully caramelized flavor. The key is patience. Don't watch the clock; watch the pan. Once it reaches the flavor zone and begins caramelizing, just a few more minutes of roasting can really return flavor dividends.

LENTIL TACOS

Taco night is always a good way to get the kids to the table. Once you get 'em there with all the crunchy excitement, topping tossing, and bright flavors, they might not even notice that theses tacos are meatless. You'll know they're packed with hearty, healthy lentils, though!

MAKES 12 TACOS

For the lentil filling

2 tablespoons (30 mL) of vegetable oil

2 onions, sliced

6 garlic cloves, sliced

1 heaping tablespoon (18 mL) of chili powder

1 teaspoon (5 mL) of ground cumin

1 cup (250 mL) of green lentils

2 cups (500 mL) of water

½ teaspoon (2 mL) of salt

½ teaspoon (2 mL) of your favorite hot sauce

For the taco toppings

A head of Bibb or iceberg lettuce

12 small soft taco shells

12 hard taco shells

A few handfuls of taco blend cheese

Your favorite salsa

A large bunch of fresh cilantro

1 or 2 limes, cut in wedges

Prepare the lentil filling first. Splash the vegetable oil into a large skillet or sauté pan over medium-high heat. Toss in the onions and garlic; sauté until the textures soften and the flavors brighten, 2 or 3 minutes. Sprinkle in the chili powder and cumin, stir the works, and continue cooking and stirring as the flavors brighten and lose any shelf-staleness, just another minute or two. Stir in the lentils, water, and salt. Bring the works to a slow, steady simmer. Cover tightly and continue slowly cooking until the lentils are tender, 35 minutes or so. Stir in the hot sauce.

Assemble the tacos. Layer a full leaf of Bibb lettuce on a soft taco shell and fold the works around a hard taco shell. This will hold the fillings in when the hard shell inevitably breaks. Fill each taco with a heaping spoonful of lentil filling. Pack with cheese, salsa, and cilantro. Serve with the lime wedges and share!

TWIST

It's easy to replace meat with legumes in taco filling. Lentils are an excellent choice, but you could also use a can of any beans, black, red, or mixed. Just drain and rinse them well and stir them into the flavor base.

MASHED SWEET POTATOES

Sweet potatoes are nutritional powerhouses. Ounce for ounce they're packed with one of the highest concentrations of micronutrients and flavor out there. This dish packs in the flavor too—sweet maple balanced with savory miso, pungent ginger, and bright edamame. **SERVES 4**

In your favorite large saucepan, whisk together the water, maple syrup, miso, and ginger. Toss in the sweet potato chunks. Cover and bring to a slow, steady simmer over medium-low heat, and simmer until the sweet potatoes are tender, about 20 minutes. Stir in the edamame, lightly mashing the sweet potatoes as you do. Serve and share!

1 cup (250 mL) of water

¼ cup (60 mL) of real maple syrup

2 tablespoons (30 mL) of miso paste

1-inch (2.5 cm) piece of frozen ginger, grated

2 large sweet potatoes (unpeeled), cut in 1-inch (2.5 cm) cubes

2 cups (500 mL) of frozen shelled edamame, thawed

--- TWIST ---

This basic stewing method works well with a wide variety of flavors, so feel free to stir in the flavor theme of your choice. Swap any spice for the ginger. The maple can easily become honey or any jam, jelly, or marmalade. Frozen green peas are a great substitute for the edamame.

BAKING

and

TREATS

BAKING & TREATS

WHOLE WHEAT BISCUITS

A basket of freshly baked biscuits is one of life's little miracles. Want to win friends and influence people? Stop reading books and start baking biscuits! With this frozen-butter method you can bypass the messy job of cutting in the fat and skip straight to incredible flavor and flaky texture. Imagine—baking the butter into the biscuit! MAKES 8 TO 12 BISCUITS, DEPENDING ON THE SIZE

3 cups (750 mL) of all-purpose flour

1 cup (250 mL) of any whole wheat flour

2 tablespoons (30 mL) of baking powder

1 teaspoon (5 mL) of salt

1 cup (250 mL) of rock-hard frozen butter

1½ cups (375 mL) of milk

Coarse finishing salt

Coarsely ground black pepper

------ **TWIST** ------
Perhaps these biscuits are so good just the way they are that you would never consider tweaking them. Perhaps their flaky, buttery deliciousness is perfect just the way it is. In which case, any creative indulgence should be focused on flavoring some more butter—butter for melting onto the biscuits. You might work miracles with 1 cup (250 mL) of soft butter, ½ cup (125 mL) of honey, maple syrup, marmalade, or brown sugar, and 1 teaspoon (5 mL) of vanilla extract.

Preheat your oven to 400°F (200°C) and turn on your convection fan if you have one. Line a baking sheet with parchment paper or a nonstick liner to minimize cleanup.

In a large bowl, whisk together the all-purpose and whole wheat flours, baking powder, and salt, evenly distributing the finer powders amidst the coarser ones. Grasp the butter and firmly grate it through the large holes of a box grater into the flour below. Working quickly, toss the flour and butter shards together with your fingers until the fat is fully distributed throughout the flour.

Pour in the milk and stir with the handle of a wooden spoon until a dough mass forms. (The handle of the spoon is gentler on the dough.) Working quickly so the heat of your hands doesn't begin to melt the butter, gently knead the dough in the bowl a few times until the dough gathers up all the flour in the bowl. Fold it over a few more times to add a bit more strength to the dough and a few more flaky layers to the biscuits.

On a lightly floured work surface, pat and roll the dough into a disc about 12 inches (25 cm) across and 1 inch (2.5 cm) thick. Cut the works into either 8 or 12 wedges. Arrange the wedges about 1 inch (2.5 cm) apart on the baking sheet. Sprinkle with the coarse salt and freshly ground pepper. Bake until light, fluffy, crispy, and golden brown, 12 to 15 minutes. As soon as you can handle them, serve and share!

HERITAGE BREAD

Few kitchen achievements rival a loaf of freshly baked hand-crafted bread. Especially when you can stir together this bread dough in 60 seconds flat and skip the hassle of kneading your arm off. Not only is this high-moisture dough easy to make, but it also allows for an overnight rest, which makes it taste dramatically better. This is the bread I bake for my family every day. MAKES 1 LARGE LOAF

In a large bowl, whisk together the all-purpose and whole wheat flours, oats, salt, and yeast, evenly distributing the finer powders amidst the coarser ones. Measure in the water, and with the handle of a wooden spoon, thoroughly and vigorously stir until a coarse dough forms, just a minute or two. Continue stirring with the handle until all the flour in the bowl is gathered up into an evenly mixed dough ball, a few minutes more. (I usually do this step after dinner.)

Cover the bowl with drum-tight plastic wrap. Let the dough rest overnight on the kitchen counter. Just by combining flour and water, elastic gluten will automatically form and continue to strengthen within the dough. In 8 to 12 hours or so, the dough will have bubbled and doubled, and long, elastic gluten strands will have formed without any laborious kneading.

The next morning, preheat your oven to 425°F (220°C) and turn on your convection fan if you have one. Lightly oil a large loaf pan.

Uncover and marvel at your risen dough. Lightly dust the dough with flour. Gather the works up from the edges and flip it over. Roll it into a rectangle and transfer it to the loaf pan, gently and evenly encouraging it into the corners. Let the dough rest, uncovered, until it doubles and precariously rises well above the rim of the pan, another 1 to 2 hours or so, more than enough time to preheat the oven and more than enough time to forget to preheat the oven. Gently and gingerly transfer the pan to the oven and bake for precisely 45 minutes. Immediately remove the loaf from the pan so the bottom doesn't get soggy. Let it rest on a rack. As soon as it's cool enough to handle, serve and share!

3 cups (750 mL) of all-purpose or bread flour

1 cup (250 mL) of Red Fife or any other whole wheat flour

½ cup (125 mL) of old-fashioned rolled oats or multigrain hot cereal blend such as Red River Cereal

2 teaspoons (10 mL) of salt

½ heaping teaspoon (3 mL) of active dry yeast

2¼ cups (550 mL) of warm water

TWIST

There are many, many ways to freestyle your own ideas into this bread. The whole wheat flour, for instance. Reduce the white flour by 1 cup (250 mL) and add another cup of whole wheat for an even more rustic bread. Or drop the whole wheat entirely and add an equivalent amount of more white for a more refined bread. The oats or grains are really just a garnish for the dough; any porridge-style cereal blend works. My go-to favorite is the organic St. John Valley Cereal from Speerville Flour Mill in New Brunswick, speervilleflourmill.ca. Wheat bran, wheat germ, and cornmeal are great too.

SPARKLE COOKIES

Every now and then you stumble onto a bit of perfection. Years ago my buddy, renowned Vancouver pastry chef Thomas Haas, introduced me to these cookies. I promptly introduced them to everyone I know—they've been a staple in my holiday gift baskets ever since—and now I'm proudly telling the world: these are the best cookies I've ever baked. Thanks, Thomas, for sharing them! MAKES ABOUT 60 COOKIES

1 pound (450 g) of bittersweet chocolate, chopped

½ cup (125 mL) of butter, at room temperature

1 teaspoon (5 mL) of vanilla extract

1 teaspoon (5 mL) of pure orange extract

4 eggs

1 cup (250 mL) of sugar, plus more for rolling

2 cups (500 mL) of ground almonds

2 tablespoons (30 mL) of cocoa powder

------- **TWIST** -------

Remember the old days when chefs wouldn't give out their recipes and there was always a secret ingredient or two anyway? Not anymore! Now we're happy to share and we're happy when you make our recipes your own by stirring in your own ideas. These cookies may have been created in Thomas Haas's pastry shop, then tweaked and simplified a bit in mine, but ultimately they become yours as soon as you bake them once.

Set up a double boiler to melt the chocolate while insulating it from direct, damaging heat by placing a large heatproof bowl over a smaller pot of barely simmering water. Put the chocolate and butter in the bowl and gently stir the works until the chocolate is completely melted and the mixture is smooth and shiny. Stir in the vanilla and orange extracts, then remove the bowl from over the water.

Toss the eggs and sugar into a large bowl and beat with an electric mixer on the highest speed until the sugar is smoothly dissolved and the mixture thickens dramatically into smooth ribbons that fall from the beater, no more than 10 minutes. In a separate bowl, whisk together the ground almonds and cocoa powder.

Pour the egg mixture over the chocolate mixture, then sprinkle with the almond mixture. Fold the works together with a rubber spatula until everything is evenly combined. Cover and refrigerate until thoroughly chilled and firm, several hours or even overnight.

Preheat your oven to 325°F (160°C) and turn on your convection fan if you have one. Line a baking sheet or two with parchment paper or a nonstick liner.

Pour a little sugar into a shallow dish. Scoop out tablespoonfuls of the dough and roll them into 1-inch (2.5 cm) balls. Toss the balls in the sugar, evenly coating them with sparkly bits. Arrange 1 inch (2.5 cm) apart on the baking sheet. Bake for 10 to 12 minutes. They'll slump a bit and crisp on the outside but the inside will stay delightfully fudgy. Transfer to racks to cool. As soon as they're cool enough to handle, cram a few in—strictly for quality-control purposes—then serve and share!

TREE FRUIT COMPOTE

Few desserts are tastier—or easier—than ripe tree fruit soaked in a simple spiced sugar syrup. When your local fruit is at its best, that's the time to capture its flavors by simply simmering them with sugar. SERVES 4, WITH LEFTOVERS

Pour the wine, sugar, and vanilla into a large pot over medium heat. Sprinkle in your choice of spice and bring the works to a slow, steady simmer.

Meanwhile, cut the unpeeled fruit into large chunks, discarding any core or pits. Add the fruit to the simmering syrup. Simmer, stirring gently and checking progress frequently, until the aromatic syrup softens and tenderizes the fruit, permeating it with flavor. This will take just a few minutes or as long as 30, depending on the type and ripeness of the fruit.

This compote is delicious freshly made but it's even better once it cools down and refrigerates overnight. Once the syrup thickens and the flavors blend, this treat is perfect ladled over ice cream or a slice of cake. Serve and share!

2 cups (500 mL) of full-bodied Chardonnay or your favorite wine

1 cup (250 mL) of sugar

1 teaspoon (5 mL) of vanilla extract

1 heaping teaspoon (6 mL) of your favorite baking spice, such as cinnamon, nutmeg, star anise, ground cloves, ground allspice, ground cardamom, even rosemary

2 to 3 pounds (900 g to 1.35 kg) of ripe plums, peaches, apricots, nectarines, apples, cherries, or pears

---

TWIST

Tree fruit tend to be fairly firm once ripe and are thus able to absorb a bit of heating and simmering, but what about delicate berries? Try tossing a pint or two of ripe, fragrant berries in at the last second, then refrigerate the works straight away. Raspberries, blackberries, strawberries, and blueberries are all delicious in this compote.

APPLE RAISIN WALNUT PUDDING

Here's how it works. Make dinner. Mix this pudding together in 5 minutes flat. Put it in the oven. Eat dinner. When you're done, so is this delicious dessert—and it even makes its own sauce. Too easy! SERVES 6 TO 8

For the pudding

½ cup (125 mL) of milk

1 teaspoon (5 mL) of white vinegar

1 teaspoon (5 mL) of vanilla extract

½ cup (125 mL) of raisins

1 cup (250 mL) of all-purpose flour

¼ cup (60 mL) of dark brown sugar

2 teaspoons (10 mL) of baking powder

1 teaspoon (5 mL) of cinnamon

1 small apple (unpeeled), diced

½ cup (125 mL) of walnuts

For the built-in sauce

2 cups (500 mL) of apple cider, apple or orange juice, or water

2 tablespoons (30 mL) of butter

1 cup (250 mL) of brown sugar

1 teaspoon (5 mL) of your favorite baking spice (optional)

Preheat your oven to 350°F (180°C) and turn on your convection fan if you have one.

Begin with the pudding. In a small bowl, stir together the milk, vinegar, and vanilla, then toss in the raisins. Let the works rest for a few minutes while the raisins plump a bit and you get the rest of the pudding ready.

In a large bowl, whisk together the flour, brown sugar, baking powder, and cinnamon. Stir in the apples and walnuts. Pour in the milk mixture, switch to a wooden spoon, and stir the works into a smooth batter with a few swift strokes. Pour the batter into a large baking pan, allowing it to slump but not encouraging it into the corners.

Make the sauce. Pour the cider into a small pot and bring it to a boil. Turn off the heat and whisk in the butter, brown sugar, and spice (if using). Gently pour the hot sauce around the mound of pudding, forming a moat of sorts. As the pudding bakes the sauce will puddle and pool and yield delicious results. Bake until the pudding is floating in goodness, firm, and a toothpick inserted in the center comes out clean, about 30 minutes. Serve and share!

---- **TWIST** ----

If you enjoy your time in the pastry kitchen and are ready to take it up a notch, try experimenting with your baking spices a bit. Get to know their flavors—cinnamon, nutmeg, allspice, cloves, cardamom, anise, ginger, mace, juniper, coriander, fennel, lavender, licorice, saffron, star anise. Learn their personality. Start with two, one in the pudding and one in the sauce. Spices are strong and thus tend to be mutually complementary yet retain their distinct aromatic character. Give it a try and see what you find!

TROPICAL FRUIT CRISP

I grew up in apple country, and I've been eating (and later baking) apple oatmeal crisps since I could walk, so it didn't take me long to create this island version when I washed ashore as a Caribbean chef. This dish was an immediate and bona fide hit on my dessert menu. The flavors and fruit may be different but it's still an apple oatmeal crisp to me! SERVES 4 TO 6

Preheat your oven to 375°F (190°C) and turn on your convection fan if you have one. Lightly oil an 8-inch (2 L) square baking dish.

Craft the filling. In a medium bowl, combine the mangoes, bananas, brown sugar, and lime zest and juice. Toss until the works are well mixed and the sugar has dissolved onto the fruit. Sprinkle on the flour and toss just until evenly combined. Pile the works into the baking dish and spread evenly.

Create the topping. In a medium bowl, whisk together the flour, coconut, brown sugar, and nutmeg, evenly distributing the textures and flavors. Drizzle with the melted butter and mix the works together with your fingers, forming a crumbly topping. Sprinkle evenly over the fruit mixture. Bake until bubbly and golden brown, 30 to 45 minutes.

Put the toasted coconut in a bowl. Scoop the ice cream into small balls and roll them in the crispy coconut. Nestle alongside spoonfuls of the warm crisp. Serve and share!

For the filling

3 ripe mangoes, peeled and diced

4 bananas, cut in chunks

½ cup (125 mL) of brown sugar

The zest and juice of 1 lime

¼ cup (60 mL) of all-purpose flour

For the topping

1 cup (250 mL) of all-purpose flour

1 cup (250 mL) of sweetened shredded coconut

1 cup (250 mL) of brown sugar

1 teaspoon (5 mL) of nutmeg

½ cup (125 mL) of butter, melted

For serving

1 cup (250 mL) or so of toasted flaked coconut

Your favorite vanilla ice cream

TWIST

If you can imagine the creative thread connecting this dish to an old-fashioned apple oatmeal crisp, then you can imagine the ideas along the way. With these basic measures, a baking dish, and a hot oven, you can reliably produce a delicious fruit crisp with whatever ingredients and ideas you have lying around.

BROWN BUTTER TARTS

Can you monkey with a classic? Is it allowed? Sure, but be prepared to justify your actions. Argue that brown butter has ten times more flavor than plain melted butter. Affirm that anyone can make plain pastry, but you prefer nutmeg-scented *butter* pastry. Assert that the corn syrup in normal butter tarts is bland, that maple syrup is much tastier. Stand your ground and watch as the end justifies the means. MAKES 24 TARTS

For the pastry

3 cups (750 mL) of all-purpose flour

1 cup (250 mL) of sugar

1 teaspoon (5 mL) of freshly grated nutmeg

½ teaspoon (2 mL) of salt

1 cup (250 mL) of rock-hard frozen butter

½ cup (125 mL) of ice water

For the filling

2 cups (500 mL) of butter

1 cup (250 mL) of real maple syrup

1 cup (250 mL) of brown sugar

4 teaspoons (20 mL) of vanilla extract

4 eggs

¼ cup (60 mL) of all-purpose flour

Preheat your oven to 450°F (230°C) and turn on your convection fan if you have one. Lightly oil a standard muffin pan.

First make the pastry. In a large bowl whisk together the flour, sugar, nutmeg, and salt, evenly distributing the finer powders amidst the coarser ones. Grasp the butter and firmly grate it through the large holes of a box grater into the flour below. Working quickly, toss the flour and butter shards together with your fingers until the fat is evenly distributed throughout the flour. The cold, separate pieces will yield dividends in flavor and texture as the butter creates flaky layers of pastry.

Sprinkle the ice water into the works and stir into a dough mass with the handle of a wooden spoon. Working quickly so the heat of your hands doesn't begin to melt the butter, knead the works a few times until the dough gathers up all the flour in the bowl. Fold it over a few more times to add a bit more strength to the dough and a few more flaky layers to the pastry.

Flour your hands, the dough, the work surface, and a rolling pin. Roll the pastry out into a circle about 15 inches (38 cm) wide and ¼ inch (5 mm) thick. Using a 3½-inch (9 cm) cookie cutter (or an empty 19-ounce/540 mL can with both ends removed, or the ring from a wide-mouth canning jar), cut circles from the pastry, as many as you can. Form a pleat along one side and fit the pastry into the muffin cups, evenly filling each cup right to the rim. Gather up the remaining dough, roll out, and repeat.

Continued

Now craft the filling. Brown the butter by melting it in a saucepan, then keep on cooking it, swirling gently. Eventually the moisture in the butter will heat, steam, foam, and evaporate away. Once that moisture is gone, the butter fat left behind can rise in temperature—past the boiling point of water—into the browning, flavoring zone. Take it as far as you dare—the deeper the color, the deeper the flavor—but be ready. The line between brown and burnt black is crossed quickly, and turning off the heat to stop the cooking isn't enough. Pouring in the maple syrup will do the trick, though. Let cool for 10 minutes.

Whisk together the brown sugar, vanilla, and eggs, then whisk into the butter. Lastly, stir in the flour.

Evenly divide the filling among the pastry shells. Bake until the pastry is beautifully browned and the filling is partially set but still a bit runny, about 12 minutes. Cool slightly until you can remove the tarts from the pan. Serve and share!

- - - - - - - - - - - - - - **TWIST** - - - - - - - - - - - - -

It's easy to assume that recipes are written in stone, that a dish can't change because "that's the way it's always been done." It's also easy to see cooking as an opportunity to stir your own personality into your food. The key is to be present, to be watchful, to smell and taste and absorb as many of the clues in front of you as you can. It won't happen overnight, but eventually you'll feel confident enough to spot an opportunity and dream up a twist of your own.

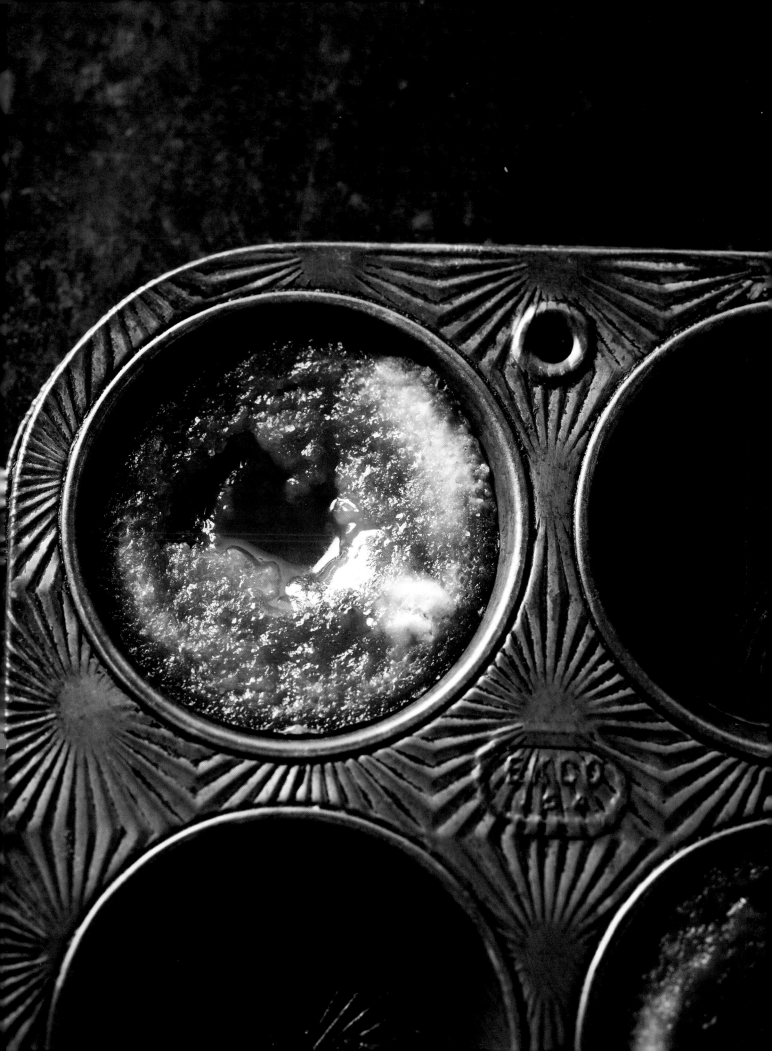

PUMPKIN PIE TARTS

Can you make a butter tart taste like a pumpkin pie? Yes! These tarts evolved from basic butter tarts, but they've come so far that they're really more like little mini pumpkin pies. But does it really matter where they came from? It's where they're heading that counts. In this case, your table! MAKES 24 TARTS

1 recipe for tart pastry (page 234)

For the filling

A 28-ounce (796 mL) can of pure pumpkin purée (not pie filling)

4 eggs, lightly beaten

2 cups (500 mL) of brown sugar

1 cup (250 mL) of butter, melted

2 teaspoons (10 mL) of vanilla extract

¼ cup (60 mL) of all-purpose flour

1 tablespoon (15 mL) of grated frozen ginger

1 tablespoon (15 mL) of freshly grated nutmeg

1 tablespoon (15 mL) of cinnamon

1 teaspoon (5 mL) of ground allspice

1 teaspoon (5 mL) of ground cloves

For the crumble topping

1 cup (250 mL) of all-purpose flour

1 cup (250 mL) of pumpkin seeds

1 cup (250 mL) of brown sugar

½ cup (125 mL) of butter, melted

Preheat your oven to 450°F (230°C) and turn on your convection fan if you have one. Lightly oil a standard muffin pan.

Make the pastry according to the instructions on page 234, grating in a whole nutmeg instead of just 1 teaspoon. Roll it out and cut it as described and line the muffin cups.

Next, craft the filling. In a large bowl, combine the pumpkin, eggs, sugar, butter, vanilla, flour, ginger, nutmeg, cinnamon, allspice, and cloves. Whisk together until smooth. Evenly fill the pastry shells.

Make the crumble topping. In a medium bowl, use your fingers to toss together the flour, pumpkin seeds, and brown sugar. Drizzle with the butter and mix the works evenly until a light, crumbly topping forms. Top each tart with its fair share.

Bake until the pastry is beautifully browned and the filling cooks through and puffs slightly, about 20 minutes. Cool slightly until you can remove the tarts from the pan. Serve and share!

TWIST

In cooking, one idea can lead to another and another. A pumpkin pie theme leads to lots of aromatic baking spices and pumpkin purée, which together call for a crisp topping. And what better to top pumpkin pie tarts with than pumpkin seeds?

APPLE CINNAMON FRITTERS

This classic country fair treat delivers the same flavors as homemade doughnuts but without the hassle. Fritter batters are easy to make and spectacularly delicious. This is the sort of treat you haul out after you've served calves' liver or burnt dinner or the like—to rebuild your reputation! MAKES 20 OR SO FRITTERS

Make the cinnamon sugar first. Simply whisk together the sugar and cinnamon in a medium bowl. Set aside.

For the fritters, pour the buttermilk into your blender or food processor; crack in the eggs. Pulse until smooth, just a moment or two. Add the flour, brown sugar, cinnamon, baking powder, and salt. Blend the works into a smooth batter. Let the batter rest for 15 minutes or so, allowing the stressed-out gluten to relax and tenderize.

While the batter rests, melt the lard in your favorite high-sided skillet or large pot over medium-high heat. For best results you'll need a pool about 1 inch (2.5 cm) deep or so. Heat the lard until a deep-fat thermometer reads 365°F (185°C).

When you're ready to fry, stir the apples into the batter. Carefully drop heaping tablespoonfuls of the batter into the hot oil, being careful not to crowd the pan. Cook until golden brown and crispy on the bottom, just 1 or 2 minutes, then flip and give the same treatment to the other side. The oil will cool slightly and you may need to crank the heat to keep close to 365°F (185°C). When the fritters are crispy and dark brown on both sides, carefully remove them with a skimmer or slotted spoon, toss them in the cinnamon sugar until evenly coated, then transfer to paper towels. Bring the fat back up to its optimum temperature before repeating with the remaining batter. Serve and share!

For the cinnamon sugar
½ cup (125 mL) of sugar
2 tablespoons (30 mL) of cinnamon

For the fritters
1 cup (250 mL) of buttermilk
2 eggs
1½ cups (375 mL) of all-purpose flour
½ cup (125 mL) of brown sugar
1 tablespoon (15 mL) of cinnamon
2 teaspoons (10 mL) of baking powder
½ teaspoon (2 mL) of salt
1 pound (450 g) of lard (or 2 to 3 cups/500 to 750 mL vegetable oil)
2 green apples (unpeeled), cut in small dice

TWIST

Feel free to try this treat with bananas and nutmeg instead of apples and cinnamon. Simply substitute 2 teaspoons (10 mL) of nutmeg for the cinnamon and chop 2 bananas instead of the apples. See which version your table prefers and see if you can dream up another!

BANANA RUM BREAD PUDDING

A simple bread pudding is one of the easiest treats to get into the oven and onto the table. It's easy for a few flavors to tag along as well, because once you've mastered the basic recipe you can easily freestyle your own ideas into the works. SERVES 8

For the bread pudding
4 eggs
1 cup (250 mL) of milk
1 cup (250 mL) of whipping cream
¼ cup (60 mL) of any rum
1 cup (250 mL) of brown sugar
1 tablespoon (15 mL) of vanilla extract
4 ripe bananas, mashed but still chunky
1 loaf of your favorite bread, cubed

For the whipped cream
2 cups (500 mL) of whipping cream
2 tablespoons (30 mL) of sugar
1 teaspoon (5 mL) of freshly grated nutmeg
1 teaspoon (5 mL) of vanilla extract

Preheat your oven to 350°F (180°C) and turn on your convection fan if you have one. Lightly oil a 13- × 9-inch (3 L) baking dish.

To make the pudding, in a large bowl, beat the eggs. Add the milk, cream, rum, brown sugar, and vanilla. Whisk until thoroughly combined. Stir in the chunky banana. It's OK if the banana makes the works a bit lumpy. Stir in the bread cubes, evenly coating every piece with the delicious custard. Let the works rest until the bread absorbs all the custard, 10 minutes or so. Pour the mixture into the baking dish. Bake until the pudding is set and cooked through and the top is golden brown, about 40 minutes.

Meanwhile, whip the cream with the sugar, nutmeg, and vanilla until soft and pillowy.

Serve and share with mounds of whipped cream!

TWIST

Bread pudding started out as an easy way to use up stale bread, so don't feel limited in your bread choices—any average-sized loaf works. Just remember, the better the bread, the better the pudding. Experiment with different baking spices, both in the whipped cream and in the pudding. Try stirring in other fruit, like apples. Nuts work well too. And of course chocolate in its many forms can sneak in—cocoa powder or melted chocolate in the batter or chips in the pudding. Your call!

PEANUT BUTTER BROWNIES

The only thing better than a batch of warm dark chocolate brownies is a batch of the same fudgy goodness with peanut butter swirled in. It's a surprisingly simple twist to a classic batch of brownie love! MAKES 12 LARGE BROWNIES

Preheat your oven to 350°F (180°C) and turn on your convection fan if you have one. Lightly oil a 13- × 9-inch (3 L) cake pan and fit it with a piece of lightly oiled parchment paper that covers the bottom and extends up and over two of the sides.

Begin with the brownies. In a bowl, whisk together the flour, cocoa powder, baking powder, and salt. Set aside. Set up a double boiler to melt the chocolate while insulating it from direct, damaging heat by placing a large heatproof bowl over a smaller pot of barely simmering water. Put the chocolate and butter in the bowl and gently stir the works until the chocolate is completely melted and the mixture is smooth and shiny. Remove the bowl from over the water, then whisk in the eggs, sugar, and vanilla until smooth. Add the flour mixture, stirring the works until smooth yet again. Set aside.

Now craft the peanut butter swirl. In a small bowl, whisk together the peanut butter, butter, icing sugar, nutmeg, and vanilla until smooth. Sneak a taste if you like. Set aside.

Pour half of the brownie batter into the prepared pan, shaking and easing it evenly into the corners. Evenly distribute small spoonfuls of the peanut butter mixture over the chocolate batter, using about half the mixture. Top with the remaining brownie batter. Dot with the remaining peanut butter mixture. Drag a spoon handle through the peanut butter batter, adding a swirl effect to the works. Bake until a toothpick inserted in the center comes out clean, about 30 minutes. When they're cool enough to handle, cut, serve, and share!

For the brownies
1 cup (250 mL) of all-purpose flour

½ cup (125 mL) of cocoa powder

1 teaspoon (5 mL) of baking powder

½ teaspoon (2 mL) of salt

8 ounces (225 g) of bittersweet chocolate, chopped

1 cup (250 mL) of butter

4 eggs, lightly beaten

2 cups (500 mL) of brown sugar

1 tablespoon (15 mL) of vanilla extract

For the peanut butter swirl
½ cup (125 mL) of your favorite peanut butter

2 tablespoons (30 mL) of butter

¼ cup (60 mL) of icing sugar

½ teaspoon (2 mL) of nutmeg

½ teaspoon (2 mL) of vanilla extract

TWIST

Brownies are not the sort of thing to take too seriously—they're ripe for experimenting. Try skipping the peanut butter and instead adding a layer of broken-up Skor bars or your favorite candy bar to the middle. Or bake the brownie batter in small terracotta flowerpots and top with cookie crumb dirt and gummi worms.

TOASTED MARSHMALLOW MILKSHAKE

See what happens when you relax in the kitchen and try out your own ideas, no matter how crazy? I mean, *imagine* **browning and toasting an entire bag of mini marshmallows under your broiler, then tossing them into a milkshake. Sheer madness. Now stop imagining and do it!** SERVES 4 TO 6 (IF YOU FEEL LIKE SHARING)

A 1-pound (450 g) bag of mini marshmallows

2 cups (500 mL) of milk

6 to 8 large scoops of your favorite vanilla ice cream

1 teaspoon (5 mL) of vanilla extract

Set an oven rack on the bottom shelf and remove any other racks. Preheat your broiler.

Spread the marshmallows out evenly on a large baking sheet. Place the pan on the bottom shelf and broil until puffed, golden brown, and melting, 6 or 8 minutes. Watch closely—the secret is to brown them as much as possible without blackening.

Add the milk, ice cream, vanilla, and half of the marshmallows to your blender and process until a smooth, thick milkshake forms. Add the remaining marshmallows and give the works a final buzz. Pour into glasses, serve, and share!

TWIST

You can't improve on perfection, but if you happen to have a bit of true orange extract around, just a splash or two will magically transform a blender full of this shake into a delicious creamsicle milkshake!

THANKS

For more than fifteen years I've enjoyed the ride of a lifetime with my shows and recipes. Along the way I've collaborated with many talented folks and made many genuine friends. I'm thankful for all our time together . . .

For my dedicated management team: Maureen for her cheerful insight and Vanessa for always being one step ahead of us all. Edna for counting all those beans and lentils.

For our hardworking video production team: Adam for his creative vision, Ann for her leadership, Jenna for her persistence, Laura for her calculator, Dean for lighting my house like the Caribbean sun, Rob for shouldering that heavy camera all day long, Dan for hearing everything yet nothing, Jonny, Graham, Cathy, Patti, Matt, Greg, Rebecca, Robbie, Ryan, and Andy. Cara for cooking real food for us all and Peter, Allan, and Marc for cleaning up our digital mess long after we're gone.

For our dedicated cookbook team: Ryan for his incredible eye for flavor and light. Madeline, whose prop collection puts a hundred-mile yard sale to shame. Noah for knowing where to put the crumbs and drips. Melanie and Sarah for reminding us all that it's still just food!

For my longtime business partner Gretha: after fifteen years we're still saying "Cheers," so we must be doing something right!

And most important, for my family: to the love of my life, Chastity, to Gabe, Ariella, and Camille. You inspire me every day to be my best in life—and in the kitchen.

INDEX

POTATOES
    with bacon and cheese, 202
    baked with cheese (cracked), 201
    cracked, 201
    french fries, spiced, 198
    mashed, variations, 197
POULTRY. See chicken
pumpkin pie tarts, 238

Q

QUINOA
    tomato basil salad, 25

R

RICE
    risotto, bacon and blue cheese, 206
    risotto, basic, 205
RISOTTO
    bacon and blue cheese, 206
    barley and asparagus, 209
    basic, 205

S

SALAD DRESSINGS. See dressings: salad
SALADS
    arugula, with goat cheese
        and pears, 22
    beef, Asian, 86
    Caesar, 6
    chickpea, tomato and cucumber, 21
    full-meal, 9
    garden, 4
    green apple, 17
    kale, white bean and cranberry, 18
    spinach and lentil sprouts, 13
    steakhouse, 10
    sweet-and-sour fennel slaw, 29
    sweet potato, 26
    sweet potato, cilantro and bean
        sprout, 48
    tomato basil quinoa, 25
SALMON
    with Asian flavours, 139
    with bacon clam chowder, 123
    in a bag, 127
SALSA. See sauces/salsa
SAUCES/SALSA
    basil Boursin, 151
    butternut squash, 172
    cheese, for lobster lasagna, 159–60
    cocktail, for poached shrimp, 119
    criolla, 65

red wine mustard, 116
tomato caper relish, 128
tomato for spaghetti, 144–47
SCALLOPS
    with tomato caper relish, 128
SCAMPI
    bacon garlic, 116
SEAFOOD. See also fish
    bacon clam chowder, 123
    lobster lasagna, 159–60
    mussels, steamed, 132
    salmon, with bacon clam
        chowder, 123
    salmon, with tomato sauce, 124
    salmon in a bag, 127
    scallops with tomato caper relish, 128
    scampi, bacon garlic, 116
    shrimp cocktail, 119
    shrimp shots, 120
SHRIMP. See also scampi
    cocktail, 119
    saffron shots, 120
SOUPS
    bacon clam chowder, 123
    hot-and-sour broth with Asian
        noodles, 164
    Thai chicken broth, 48
SPAETZLE
    whole wheat with spinach, 171
SPAGHETTI
    and tomato sauce, 144–47
SPINACH
    lasagna, 163
    and lentil salad, 13
    nutmeg, 185
    pesto, 156
    and whole wheat spaetzle, 171
STEAKS
    Brazilian grilled, 65
    burritos, 70
    iron, 65
STEWS
    beef pot pie, 73–74
    cranberry kale, 92
    mushroom, 69
SWEET POTATOES
    and cilantro and bean
        sprout salad, 48
    mash, 47
    mashed, 217
    roasted, and apples, 34–35
    salad, 26

T

TACOS
    lentils, 214
TARTS
    brown butter, 234–36
    pumpkin pie, 238
TOMATO
    and basil carbonara, 155
    basil quinoa salad, 25
    cherry, and caper relish, 128
    cherry, and pan-roasted zucchini, 182
    and chickpea and cucumber salad, 21
    meaty sauce, 78
    roasted, 34–35
    roasted, and pasta, 148
    sauce, and salmon, 124
    sauce, for lobster lasagna, 159–60
    sauce for spaghetti, 144–47

V

VINAIGRETTE. See dressings: salad

W

WHEAT BERRIES
    pilaf, 210
WHISKEY
    and bacon jam, 104
WHITEFISH
    pan-fried, 131

Z

ZUCCHINI
    pan-roasted and cherry tomatoes, 182